ETHNICITY, LAW AND THE SOCIAL GOOD

* * * * *

VOLUME II

ETHNICITY AND
PUBLIC POLICY
SERIES

ETHNICITY, LAW AND THE SOCIAL GOOD

WINSTON A. VAN HORNE
EDITOR

THOMAS V. TONNESEN
MANAGING EDITOR

UNIVERSITY OF WISCONSIN SYSTEM
AMERICAN ETHNIC STUDIES COORDINATING
COMMITTEE/ URBAN CORRIDOR CONSORTIUM

University of Wisconsin System American Ethnic Studies
Coordinating Committee/Urban Corridor Consortium
P. O. Box 413, Milwaukee, WI 53201

International Standard Book Number ISBN 0-942672-02-X (cloth)
International Standard Book Number ISBN 0-942672-03-8 (paper)
Library of Congress Catalog Card Number: 83-80442

UNIVERSITY OF WISCONSIN SYSTEM AMERICAN ETHNIC STUDIES COORDINATING COMMITTEE

DR. WINSTON A. VAN HORNE
    University of Wisconsin–Milwaukee
    Chairperson, AESCC

DR. PETER J. KELLOGG
    University of Wisconsin–Green Bay

DR. LIONEL A. MALDONADO
    University of Wisconsin–Parkside

DR. WILLIAM J. MURIN
    Director, Urban Corridor Consortium

DR. MELVIN C. TERRELL
    University of Wisconsin–Oshkosh

MR. THOMAS V. TONNESEN
    Program Coordinator, AESCC (ex officio)

The University of Wisconsin System American Ethnic Studies Coordinating Committee (AESCC) wishes to acknowledge the contributions of its former members, as well as those of the Urban Corridor Consortium Steering Committee and the University of Wisconsin System American Ethnic Studies Advisory Committee.

PREFACE

More than fifteen hundred years ago, St. Augustine exclaimed "O Truth, Truth! how inwardly . . . did the marrow of my soul pant . . . after Thee Thyself, the Truth, with whom is no variableness, neither shadow of turning." (*The Confessions*, III, 6). The Truth after which Augustine's soul panted is fixed, immutable, incorrigible and external—the Truth (God) of *Civitas Dei*. But there is another truth, the truth of *civitas terrae*, which is changeable, mutable, corrigible and time-bound. It is this truth, which is but a shadow of the Truth, that guides the everyday activities of man. It is truth, not the Truth, that structures human law and determines the social good. But truth strives to be coeval with the Truth, and in its becoming it changes human law and the social good ceaselessly. The dynamics of truth thus energize both the law and the social good, whose continuous motion would come to rest only if they were to become one with Truth—at which point they would cease to be.

The dynamic qualities of the law, the social good and their relations are presented in the following essays in the context of ethnic group interests. Each interest, explicitly or implicitly, makes claims upon truth as it strives to organize a particular relation between the law and the social good. However, given the constant becoming of truth, there are many conceptions of truth, and these reinforce the diversity of ethnic group interests. This diversity sometimes occasions conflict, at other times fosters cooperation, and at still other times promotes competition. The essays in this volume make clear that there is no one Truth that grounds the variety of ethnic group interests so that all would be satisfied with a given relation between the law and the social good.

It is obvious from even a cursory reading of these essays that dogmatism, clericalism, parochialism and philistinism by both the individual *qua* individual, the individual *qua* ethnic group, and ethnic group *qua* ethnic group disserve the law as well as the social good. Both the law and the good of the society must be amenable to diverse conceptions of truth and divergent group interests. If this were ever to be otherwise, the society would soon fragment around the fissures wrought by contradictory, conflicting and competing ethnic group interests. The scholars whose works are presented here leave us with the clear and distinct impression that the strength, promise and hope of

American society are to be found in the tolerance of multiple truths, which makes possible different uses of the law to promote the social good that is but an image of the Truth. Should such tolerance dissipate universally to the point where the Truth of the law and the social good were to be deemed *one* with the truth of a particular ethnic group's interests, the society would no doubt lose what many believe to be a source of incalculable strength.

The University of Wisconsin System American Ethnic Studies Coordinating Committee is gratified by the reputation that its Green Bay Colloquium on Ethnicity and Public Policy has achieved in four short years, and by the success of *Ethnicity and Public Policy* which was published last year. The critical, tough-minded, analytical rigor, as well as sensitivity and perceptivity, that marked that volume are replicated in this book. Those who found the essays in the previous volume to be provocative, insightful and useful should be delighted by the contributions that comprise this volume.

I should like to thank each of those whose hard work made this volume possible. A special word of thanks must go to the University of Wisconsin System Administration, especially President Robert M. O'Neil, for its/his strong support of the work of the UW System American Ethnic Studies Coordinating Committee. Finally, I cannot overstate the contribution of Thomas V. Tonnesen, our Managing Editor and the AESCC's Program Coordinator, who worked closely with me in the editing of this volume.

Winston A. Van Horne

The University of Wisconsin-Milwaukee

CONTENTS

INTRODUCTION

Peter J. Kellogg

University of Wisconsin—Green Bay

This volume examines the relations between ethnicity and the law, looking first at the law and ethnicity in principle, and then at the law and ethnicity as they relate to education, employment and neighborhoods. The scholars whose works are included represent a broad spectrum of viewpoints, from those believing that the law should completely ignore ethnicity, to those advocating large-scale public programs—and perhaps even the restructuring of basic social institutions—to overcome the effects of past discrimination against members of various ethnic groups. Despite this wide diversity in the authors' views, their scholarship reveals interesting areas of possible consensus, as well as clear reasons for the remaining disagreements.

Philosophically, the papers represent at least four different perspectives on whether and how the law should consider ethnicity to promote the social good. One perspective, represented clearly by both Nathan Glazer and Raoul Berger, holds that the law should recognize only individual rights and that membership in an ethnic or racial group is a purely private matter. Glazer, for example, approves the repeal of laws such as segregation statutes that treat individuals differently on the basis of their group memberships, but he opposes measures such as court-ordered school desegregation policies because they require consideration of the individual's group identity. He would thus proscribe discrimination as well as race-conscious measures that mitigate the effects of past discrimination. Glazer insists that court involvement in education has reduced the authority of professional educators and weakened the effectiveness of American public education.

Glazer's apparent premise is that the law is the chief determiner of social equity; and if the law is impartial, then equity is—by definition—achieved. He does not see the law as simply one element in an intricate set of organic relationships constituting a social system. Nor does he attach much significance to the disabilities accumulated over centuries as the law and virtually every other element of the social system interacted to deny opportunities to particular groups. He would be satisfied if the law ceased to require discrimination, regardless of the social inequity structured into the society by previous legal, economic, political and social relationships.

From a slightly different perspective, Raoul Berger shares Glazer's emphasis on the primacy of the law. As his version of the cardinal social good, Berger stresses fidelity to a literal interpretation of the intent of the drafters of the Constitution. From his study of the drafting and debate of the Fourteenth Amendment, he concludes that the framers intended to guarantee black Americans three, and only three, rights: the right to own property; the right to make contracts; and the right to have access to the courts. Since, in Berger's judgment, no other rights were intended by the drafters of the Fourteenth Amendment, any effort to interpret that amendment as guaranteeing other rights—even non-segregated education—would be judicial usurpation and replacement of the rule of law with judicial tyranny. He observes that the political society of the United States when the Fourteenth Amendment was drafted and ratified was intensely racist. For example, Senator John Sherman is quoted as saying, "We do not like Negroes. We do not conceal our dislike." George Julian also represented the attitude of the time when he remarked, "The real trouble is we hate the Negro." Believing such racism to be part of the attitudes and intent of those who drafted the amendment, Berger insists that the Fourteenth Amendment neither proscribes public racism nor even guarantees black Americans equal citizenship. In his view, if Americans want equal rights for blacks, they should amend the Constitution to say so; otherwise, judicial interpretations requiring equal rights are usurpation of legislative power by the courts, and such interpretations should be overturned.

Berger believes that the Court of the 1930s departed from strict construction to undermine the New Deal, and he is anxious to avoid any such abuses in the future. His insistence on the primacy of a literal reading of the Constitution presumably implies that the law should recognize only individuals, not ethnic groups—a concern also central to Glazer. However, Berger departs from Glazer drastically by implying that a second-class citizenship for black Americans is permissible because the Constitution does not specifically empower the federal government to guarantee equal rights for blacks beyond the stated rights of property, contract and access to the courts. This devotion to the abstract principle of strict construction as the highest social good, regardless of other social goods, could result in traumatic attempts to wrench American blacks back into subordinate status, unless the Constitution were amended to say what the Fourteenth Amendment has been understood to say for many years. In principle, Berger would allow no remedy for persecuted minorities, save appeal to the good will of the majority. Such an appeal might well prove futile. Furthermore, this approach ignores the fundamental principle, basic to this nation's Constitution and Bill of Rights, that the Constitution protects minorities against popular persecutors.

To summarize this first perspective, then, Berger and Glazer perceive somewhat different abstract legal principles as the highest social good. For different reasons, each believes that the law should accommodate no consideration of group membership and should recognize neither race nor ethnicity—except for Berger's rather extreme acceptance that federal law could tolerate diminished rights for some. In contrast to these views, each of the other essays advocates that the law recognize race and/or ethnicity, in some measure, to compensate for past wrongs.

Compensatory recognition of ethnic identity constitutes the second of the four perspectives represented by the essays. Robert O'Neil analyzes the current status of affirmative action programs, particularly in the field of higher education. He concludes that such measures have brought significant progress resulting, for example, in nearly proportional college attendance for black Americans in traditional college-age groups. However, he sees a widespread assault on affirmative action materializing on several fronts. Through careful analysis of the *Bakke* decision and other Supreme Court opinions, O'Neil concludes that the Court will allow, but not require, a variety of race-conscious college admission programs. O'Neil also observes that the Court has been less activist than commonly pictured, waiting until passage of the Civil Rights Act of 1964 to address public accommodations, for example. He views affirmative action as an important mechanism for overcoming past inequities, as well as for achieving diversity and educating professionals to meet the needs of otherwise underserved communities. Despite the Court's sanction of some forms of affirmative action, O'Neil is not optimistic about the future of affirmative action policies, at least in education. He notes the declining number of minority students in higher education and hopes that enough progress has already been made through affirmative action to ensure that an untimely end to such policies would not have an irrevocably negative impact.

Although O'Neil discusses the compensatory recognition of ethnic status most directly, Marable, Pondrom, Kellogg and Krickus also call for various forms of public policy to compensate for past discrimination. Manning Marable provides detailed information on the employment and economic status of American black women today, revealing massive poverty and low income for many of those who do hold jobs. He attacks the notions that black women have been making rapid progress or that they have gained at the expense of black men. He suggests several governmental programs to accommodate the special needs of women who are poor or are heads of households, including counseling, training, day care, expanded food stamp programs and protection for those engaged in union organizing. Because these programs are intended to benefit both minority and white working-class women with particular needs, Marable's suggestions confront economic disadvantages and sex discrimination, as well as racial discrimination. His emphasis is on overcoming economic disadvantages among women in all groups, but his data demonstrate the disproportionate needs for such compensatory assistance programs among America's black women. He argues for compensatory programs, but extends their target populations beyond just racial or ethnic groups to include all the economically deprived. Marable's approach would meet urgent needs of minority groups, as well as of low-income whites; and by targeting all people in economic need, he may thus overcome many of the negative attitudes in some public and scholarly circles created by programs designed only to benefit minorities. His suggestions might indeed satisfy both Glazer's call for color-blind policies and Berger's narrow interpretation of the Fourteenth Amendment.

Cyrena Pondrom makes similar proposals. Her analysis, though, is more focused on employment training and, interestingly enough, she regards affirmative action as a negative, even harmful, policy. Pondrom argues that the cause of minority poverty is a lack of skills, and she advocates government-sponsored training programs, such as CETA, to "improve human capital." Pondrom apparently believes that the labor market is essentially color-blind and that all people with needed skills will find jobs. Furthermore, she argues that affirmative action has benefited only middle-class minorities, not the poor. She gives a detailed analysis of vocational programs to show that they significantly increase earnings and regularity of employment, and that such gains increase over time. The "carrot" of increasing skills that employers value is better than the "stick" of prosecution for discrimination, she argues, advocating carefully targeted programs aimed at economic and educational disadvantages. Her programs would be color-blind in principle, but her data show that at least half the participants in such programs have been minorities. Thus, her proposals for targeted vocational training parallel Marable's broader recommendations. Both approaches would compensate for past discrimination by providing government support to the economically disadvantaged, with the expectation that minorities, disproportionally disadvantaged, would benefit disproportionally.

Kellogg and Krickus also call for government action to compensate for past discrimination. Both see a complex urban system in which government and private interests have combined to favor the well-to-do and the suburbs at the expense of the working class and the poor, particularly ethnic groups and minorities. They point to government housing policies that have segregated the middle class from the working class, subsidized middle-class suburbs, and perverted urban renewal from a program to develop housing into one supporting commercial development (often destroying ethnic neighborhoods in the process). They also cite transportation systems that serve suburbs and shatter neighborhoods, the disinvestiture of private capital, and many other public and private policies undermining the less privileged social groups. The cumulative result is segregated cities, weakened ethnic neighborhoods, inter-group hostilities, and the perpetuation of segregation. Kellogg argues that the metropolitan system sets white ethnic groups against minorities to the disadvantage of both, and observes that all groups should cooperate to solve common systemic problems. He calls for massive government programs to revitalize neighborhoods and provide low- and moderate-income housing throughout metropolitan areas. Krickus particularly emphasizes the problems of white ethnic groups and defends them against charges of racism; but he too advocates increased government support for neighborhoods, reaffirming that both minorities and ethnic groups have been harmed or neglected by past policies. Thus, both Kellogg and Krickus advocate compensatory programs to undo past discrimination or neglect. Implicitly, those programs (like the vocational programs mentioned above) would be directed to areas of economic need and would consequently benefit minorities and certain ethnic groups disproportionally.

The third perspective on the law as it impacts ethnicity and the social good holds that ethnicity is of inherent value and that public policy should acknowledge and support ethnic diversity because a variety of ethnic cultures contributes to the social good. This view, also shared by Krickus and Kellogg, most clearly emerges in Richard Ruiz's discussion of bilingual education. Ruiz values the ability to speak more than one language, a goal educators frequently seek for their students, though with only moderate success; and Ruiz sees students whose native tongue is other than English as assets to the educational system. Both one's ability to speak a language other than English and one's appreciation of the culture represented by that additional language are assets to the person and to the nation, contributing to the social good and, Ruiz believes, deserving to be nurtured by the schools. One implication of his argument is that the schools cannot be "language-blind" or "culture-blind." They must either support the development and understanding of a student's native language and culture, or they must press for assimilation and the consequent atrophy of diverse native languages and cultures. To be educated in one's native language is not a special privilege, but rather a form of equal educational opportunity. Ruiz believes that the law should support each individual's particular culture and language and should not try to force a different language or culture on students to the exclusion of their own. Much of his analysis documents the failure of educational policymakers to appreciate the value of lingual and cultural diversity. Most legislation and policies dealing with bilingual education, he shows, regard bilingual education as transitional and compensatory, a remedial program to help students overcome a "handicap." He points to the sad irony that students fluent in a second language are referred to as "limited English speaking" because their families speak a language other than English, while a teacher whose minimal competency has led to certification in two languages is called a "bilingual" educator. Ruiz further cites a long series of court cases and public policies which have required assimilation and, as a result, have denigrated ethnic cultures. He concludes:

> What is needed are policies aimed at developing the resources which exist in ethnic communities, rather than eradicating them. This can only promote the greater "social good," since it aims at an integration of the strengths of each group. In the cases I have elected to focus on, language is to be seen as just such a resource. And as a resource, our orientation toward it should be for planning and management, always for the benefit of the greater collectivity.

Ruiz is clearly speaking for the position which not only values diversity for its own sake, but also sees it as contributing positively to the society. This view is in direct conflict with that of Glazer, who is troubled by the inherent dangers of ethnic cleavages and urges assimilation as the only way to maintain the unity of a democratic society. Berger, in discussion during the colloquium, expressed concern for ethnic diversity, but gave greater emphasis to the need for assimilation, fearing the possible development of an American Quebec. In contrast, Ruiz anticipates an opportunity to resolve the dilemma so often posed: the idea that strengthening group identity necessarily undermines social cohesion. Instead, Ruiz sees respect for, and support of, ethnic differences as strengthening the social whole and increasing loyalty to the society far more than would forced homogenization.

Krickus also argues that ethnicity is a resource which makes positive contributions to the whole society and thus should be nurtured by public policy. He laments the scholarly view held, he believes, by representatives of both the left and right—that ethnicity is a dangerous, pre-modern anachronism which retards social unity and progress. In his analysis of ethnic neighborhoods, Krickus finds rather that such ethnic social groups have been agents of stability and progress. Neighborhoods, he holds, provide a sense of community as well as jobs, business revenues, property taxes, buffer zones between the poor and the affluent, and stable social systems which provide a host of free services such as the "care of young and old people, the amelioration of antisocial behavior," and others. He urges "that policymakers begin to perceive ethnicity as an asset, not as a problem or limitation and, by their actions, acknowledge that white ethnic neighborhoods are a social good."

Krickus sees white ethnic neighborhoods as suffering from a wide range of private and public policies which shape metropolitan areas for the benefit of affluent groups that often reside in the suburbs. In this sense he shares the fourth perspective on ethnicity and the social good—the interpretation that ethnicity is a social problem because complex economic and political forces acknowledge and perpetrate ethnic and racial divisions, as well as often negatively influence these groups. This perspective, represented most clearly by Marable and Kellogg, holds that race and ethnicity can be understood only in the context of broader social forces that shape the modern city, as well as the national and even international economy.

Kellogg traces the development of residential segregation through its long history, beginning with the early separation of classes significantly bolstered by such public policies as zoning, and continuing through a host of more recent public and private actions. The result of this development is the rigid segregation of economic groups, a social fact of life now incorporated into a complex metropolitan system in which diverse public policies and subsidies benefit affluent suburbs. The poor, who are disproportionally racial minorities and white ethnic groups, are left to struggle for survival in decaying neighborhoods and financially starved cities. Race and ethnicity have become emotional symbols, Kellogg believes, but the hostilities they generate serve vested economic interests. Kellogg urges members of racial and ethnic groups to understand their common victimization and unite against the structural disadvantages inherent in the existing metropolitan system. Like Krickus, he recommends a shift in government policies to aid previously disadvantaged groups as an essential step to preserve American cities and serve the general good. Because the society is now so divided by policies which have treated individuals differently according to their respective group memberships, social unity cannot occur unless the disparities are remedied. Presumably, measures directed to assist economically defined groups, rather than racial or ethnic ones, would be a major step toward such unity, but Kellogg insists that discrimination itself must also be dispelled if other measures are to succeed.

Marable shares this fourth perspective by examining the larger dimensions of the political economy beyond simple discrimination, and he finds serious problems particularly affecting minority groups. Marable focuses the second half of his analysis on the plight of Frostbelt cities suffering from the flight of capital, and thus jobs, to the Sunbelt and the Third World. He points out that such private decisions about capital investment have disastrous consequences for many cities and population groups, and he advocates a variety of measures to attract capital back to Frostbelt cities and to quell the regional competition for jobs. Marable and Kellogg thus (and, to a lesser extent, Krickus) look beyond discrimination to the comprehensive economic structure of the society. They see ethnic and racial tensions not as a cause, but as a consequence, and each suggests a variety of ways to change basic economic policies for greater equity and social justice. Their proposals are not meant as substitutes for firm anti-discrimination measures. However, they do see the major problems of racial and ethnic minorities as stemming from fundamental economic principles and practice, and they call for measures to rectify these defects. Marable and Kellogg are adamant that matters of ethnicity and race are intimately tied to considerations of class and the democratic control of basic economic decisions.

While these four perspectives on ethnicity and the social good contain a number of apparent and real contradictions, important agreements are identifiable among them. Five of the eight essays advocate some form of economic aid targeted to economically disadvantaged groups, with the intention that the aid will particularly benefit members of racial and certain white ethnic groups. The other essays do not address those proposals directly, but the logic of their arguments does not provide any grounds for opposing such aid, unless perhaps Berger would find it unconstitutional. (His anger at the courts for undermining the New Deal, though, suggests that he would not object). Thus, the contributors exhibit some consensus for government programs to eliminate poverty and revitalize cities. There is certainly no argument that poverty or decaying cities serve the general good; there is, accordingly, substantial agreement that such problems are proper concerns of public policy. Disagreement is likely be strong, however, in a discussion of whether these problems are inherent in the structure of the American economic system or can be resolved through supplementary programs such as CETA. Marable and Pondrom would probably represent the respective poles of such a debate.

Marable and Kellogg espouse strong support for economic programs directed to economically disadvantaged groups, with the intention that minorities would particularly benefit. Such programs could be color-blind and thus not offensive to Glazer or Berger. It would be ironic, though, if Berger and Glazer were to accept public programs treating individuals as members of disadvantaged economic groups, but not as members of identifiable cultural groups, especially considering that cultural diversity could be viewed more as a national asset than a liability. This paradox reflects the difficulty of deciding the significance of group membership in a constitutional, pluralistic society.

These essays expose a sharp conflict over whether ethnicity and race are in themselves fit matters for public policy. Because some scholars see the individual as primary, they regard any consideration of group membership (and hence, any definition of rights according to groups) as a threat to the rights of individuals and to the constitutional system itself. Others believe that individuals exist and have their life opportunities determined largely as members of groups; thus, only by considering such group membership can individual rights be guaranteed, particularly when an individual's opportunities are largely shaped by generations of past discrimination against his or her group. The clearest among several representative issues in this debate is whether all children should be taught only English (i.e., the language of most individuals in the country) as a means to provide the same treatment for all, or whether each child should be taught in his or her native language as well as in English, thus recognizing as an individual right the preservation of one's language and, by extension, one's culture. Both those favoring and those opposing public recognition of diverse cultures can argue that they seek to protect the rights of individuals. The differences arise over whether an individual has a right to maintain a group culture. In a sense, those who advocate a society based on the rights of individuals rather than on the rights of groups would deny to individuals the important right of choosing to preserve their group's culture and language. Instead, they posit a social right—the right to cohesion and to common values, culture and language—for the sake of national unity, which impels them to suppress what many regard as an important individual right. This controversy is certainly defined, but hardly resolved, in this volume.

Also unresolved is the question of whether ethnic cultures are a social good, regardless of whether they are an individual right. Only Glazer addresses this question directly, and he answers it in the negative. The other contributors, with the possible exception of Berger, view ethnic diversity as a good which society has erred in ignoring or denigrating. They believe that acknowledging and developing the different strengths of each group strengthens the whole. Implicitly, these scholars assume that a heterogeneous society that respects the differences among social groups will ultimately attract greater loyalty from

the members of the individual groups comprising it. If this assumption
is accurate, their view may suggest the resolution of a long and painful
controversy in American history.

Finally, a sharp controversy among the contributors focuses on the
issue of compensatory legal recognition for groups which have been historically disadvantaged. Glazer and Berger forcefully oppose any compensatory program based on race or ethnicity, while O'Neil, Ruiz,
Marable, Krickus and Kellogg advocate a variety of such programs.
Pondrom proposes programs to compensate for past discrimination,
but favors those targeted specifically at individuals' economic needs,
disregarding ethnic identity. Her proposal accommodates much of
what Marable, Krickus and Kellogg advocate and, even in its limited
scope, it may illustrate a significant principle for partial resolution of
the debate over compensatory programs. In sharp contrast to O'Neil,
Ruiz, Marable, Kellogg and, possibly, Krickus, however, Pondrom
minimizes the significance of racial and ethnic discrimination. She con-
cedes, though, that affirmative action has brought important gains to
middle-class minorities. Thus, a substantial consensus emerges in support of economically targeted programs which would benefit members
of identifiable racial and ethnic groups, as well as other individuals.

All the contributors support anti-discrimination legislation and its
enforcement, except Berger, who would do so only under the terms of a
constitutional amendment. More forceful programs, such as affirmative action, to overcome past discrimination have the support of
O'Neil, Kellogg, Marable and Ruiz, but receive significant opposition
from Berger, Glazer and Pondrom. Krickus, too, is troubled about the
effects of such programs on white ethnic groups; he is especially concerned that because they benefit non-white ethnic groups most directly, such programs are actually socially discriminatory.

To summarize, among these broadly divergent opinions, significant
areas of potential agreement exist, particularly relating to economically targeted programs seeking social justice. A discussion of the possible forms for such programs, though, would no doubt generate intense
controversy. There is also considerable implicit agreement that economic issues—jobs, poverty, neighborhood revitalization, education,
funding vocational training, support for single heads of households,
restoration of the frost-belt economy and others—represent a high priority among the concerns of ethnic and racial groups. Some contributors firmly believe that programs to deal with economic problems
should be targeted to serve those in economic need, rather than explicitly to overcome past discrimination, as a politically effective means to
meet the needs of all who are less privileged, and to build a majority
coalition supporting such programs.

On the issue of affirmative action to undo the effects of past discrimination, the contributors divide sharply, although they all agree on proscribing further discrimination. Some fear that actions intended to reduce the effects of historic discrimination could produce hostile backlash among whites, thus dividing the groups which might otherwise unite for economic reform. These scholars imply that adequate economic programs combined with effective anti-discrimination enforcement should enable minority group members, through their individual efforts, to overcome the impact of cumulative discrimination. The great increase in college enrollments among minorities through the 1970s, for example, is attributed by some of the contributors to financial aid programs based on economic need, and thus illustrates how successful such measures can be. On the other hand, others argue that while economic programs are necessary, they are not sufficient to counterbalance the accumulated weight of discrimination. They reply to the argument about minorities' increased college enrollments by noting that, since the *Bakke* decision, undergraduate enrollments of minorities are declining by as much as 50 percent in some institutions, and that minority graduate enrollments, in which affirmative action has played a particularly important role, are dropping precipitously.

Similarly, on the broader issue of whether ethnic culture ought to be supported as a matter of right or as a contribution to the social good, the contributors differ widely. Each voices some support for the right of ethnic groups to preserve their own cultures, although some are troubled by the societal cleavages that this might foster. They are, for example, concerned that the ossification of linguistic differences might "Quebecize" the society, if we might so speak. They favor the maintenance of ethnic cultures, but only as a private matter with no governmental support. The government's neutrality in this matter is, however, difficult to imagine. With respect to educational policies regarding language, for example, if the public schools offer bilingual education, they seem to support an ethnic culture; but neither is education in English only a neutral policy, for it would tend to repress some cultures. Clearly, diverse cultures are a valuable resource which ought to be nurtured for the overall social good.

Among the contributors, as well as among divergent factions in American society itself, common support can be found for economic programs that provide a realistic basis on which diverse groups could unite. Eventually, Americans might develop a healthy mutual respect for ethnic diversity similar to the religious pluralism and tolerance which have emerged, albeit after a tedious, agonizing struggle. Unfortunately, as the processes of learning and understanding evolve, the powerful emotions inherent in controversial issues of race, ethnicity and the law may long obscure the very real areas of potential agreement. *Ethnicity, Law and the Social Good* is offered in a spirit of intellectual honesty and good will in the hope that it will help clarify areas of disagreement and illuminate areas of potential consensus in the continuing discussion of these urgent, complex social problems.

ETHNICITY AND THE LAW: THE ROLE OF THE SUPREME COURT

Raoul Berger

Charles Warren Senior Fellow Emeritus in American Legal History
Harvard University

The law that concerns ethnic groups clusters largely around judicial decisions seeking to correct past discrimination against racial minorities by preferential treatment. In his fair-minded book *Discriminating Against Discrimination*, Robert M. O'Neil observes that there is a "natural fear that if minorities are preferred . . . other groups must be 'unpreferred' to their detriment." "Someone," he comments, "must be displaced, if more minorities are admitted to a class of relatively fixed size,"[1] whether it be in higher education or employment opportunities. European ethnic groups such as Poles, Slavs, and Italians consider that they are unjustly displaced. In combination they probably equal the black community numerically, for reportedly there are twelve million people of Polish origin alone in the United States.[2]

O'Neil has correctly written that "few persons of conscience question the past deprivation of minority groups, or their exclusion from the benefits of higher education; the controversy relates to the fairness and lawfulness of remedies."[3] The "reverse discrimination" remedy was born only yesterday; O'Neil noted that as of 1975 "there was simply no decision in the hundred year history of the equal protection clause that dealt with preferential treatment or so-called reverse discrimination."[4] I would not question O'Neil's deductions from past decisions; I make what lawyers call a plea to the jurisdiction and contend that the Court is not authorized to decide such cases. The framers of the Fourteenth Amendment excluded segregation from the scope of the amendment; consequently the Court is not empowered to deal with the reverse discrimination branch of desegregation.

The preferential treatment decisions constitute but one facet of what Professor Philip Kurland of the University of Chicago described as "the usurpation by the judiciary of general governmental powers on the pretext that its authority derives from the Fourteenth Amendment."[5] An ardent advocate of judicial revisionism, Professor Paul

Brest of Stanford University, admits that "many of what we have come to regard as the irreducible minima of rights are actually supra-constitutional; almost none of the others are entailed in the text or original understanding."[6] They are, in short, judicial fabrications. The late Professor Robert G. McCloskey, another admirer of the judicial role, wrote that "during the past thirty years, the Court has built a whole body of constitutional jurisprudence in this broad field called civil liberties almost out of whole cloth."[7]

These judicial constructs merely reflect the predilections of the justices, as we may gather from Justice William O. Douglas' disclosure that "the 'gut' reactions of a judge at the level of constitutional adjudication, dealing with the vagaries of due process, freedom of speech and the like, [is] the main ingredient of his decision."[8] The people do not realize that they are governed by such "gut reactions" rather than by constitutional mandates. Professor Felix Frankfurter pointed this out to Franklin Roosevelt during the 1937 Court-packing campaign:

> People have been taught to believe that when the Supreme Court speaks it is not they who speak but the Constitution, whereas, of course, in so many vital cases, it is *they* who speak and *not* the Constitution. And I verily believe that is what the country needs most to understand.[9]

We need to understand that the justices, under the guise of interpretation, have engaged in amending the Constitution, a power reserved to the people themselves. With George Washington I urge, "Let there be no change by usurpation; for though this, in one instance, may be the instrument of good, it is the customary weapon by which free governments are destroyed."[10]

Today the Court usurps power for benign purposes but yesterday it blocked attempts to ameliorate socio-economic evils—child labor, long hours, low wages[11]—and tomorrow its influence may once more be malign. There is a deplorable tendency to reason that because a given result is laudable, the Constitution therefore confers power on the Court to accomplish it.[12] This is the sheerest wishful thinking, overlooking that the Tenth Amendment reserves all powers not granted to the federal government for the states and the people. In 1942 I wrote that I liked it no better when Justice Black read my predilections into the Constitution than when Justices Butler and McReynolds read in theirs.[13] My commitment is not to any particular result but to observance of the Constitution. Justice Cardozo, then Chief Judge of the New York Court of Appeals, declared in 1921 that when "judges ignore the mandate of a statute, and render judgment in spite of it . . . by that abuse of power they violate the law." The substitution "of the individual sense of justice," he continued, "might result in a benevolent despotism if the judges were benevolent men. It would put an end to the rule of law," a "cataclysm."[14]

Adherence to the Constitution is even more essential when departures from it plunge the Court into fierce political controversy. O'Neil observed that "one cannot overlook the highly charged political context in which the [preferential treatment] debate has been conducted," and notes that "the power to classify on the basis of race, no matter how 'benign' the goal, is always dangerous."[15] Moreover, this issue (and the related issue of busing) has been "deeply divisive" and has engendered "bitterness" among "Italians, Slavs, Poles and other Eastern European nationals."[16] Such conflicts put a great strain on the judicial process; judges were not meant to resolve heated political controversies, as we may learn from the Court's ill-fated attempt to settle the slavery issue in the *Dred Scott* case.[17]

These momentous issues cannot be addressed by *ex cathedra* pronouncements; let us then descend to the grubby details of proof. We will begin with the unmistakable exclusion of Negro suffrage from the Fourteenth Amendment, for as Richard Kluger, who rejoices in the desegregation decision, wrote, "Could it be reasonably claimed that segregation had been outlawed by the Fourteenth when the yet more basic emblem of citizenship—the ballot—had been withheld from the Negro under that amendment?"[18] Dissenting from the "one person-one vote" decisions, which tacitly postulated that the Court was given jurisdiction over suffrage, Justice Harlan reminded the Court that the decisions were "made in the face of irrefutable and still unanswered history to the contrary."[19] Professor Louis Lusky of Columbia University cited Harlan's "irrefutable and unrefuted demonstration" that the Fourteenth Amendment "was not intended to protect the right to vote."[20] There are similar expressions by apologists for an activist Court.[21] Professor Gerald Gunther of Stanford University tells us, "The ultimate justification of *Reynolds* [one person-one vote] is hard, if not impossible, to set forth in constitutionally legitimate terms. It rests, rather, on the view that courts are authorized to step in when injustices exist and other institutions fail to act. That is a dangerous—and I think, illegitimate—prescription for judicial action."[22]

But we should not rely on a mere count of noses, and so take leave to summarize a few confirmatory facts. Justice Brennan found that "seventeen or nineteen" Northern states had rejected black suffrage between 1865 and 1868.[23] Consequent to that rejection, Roscoe Conkling, a member of the Joint Committee on Reconstruction, which drafted the Fourteenth Amendment, said that it would be "futile to ask three quarters of the States to do . . . the very thing which most of them have already refused to do . . . ."[24] Another member of the committee, Senator Jacob Howard, spoke to the same effect.[25] Senator William Fessenden, chairman of the Joint Committee, said of a suffrage proposal that there was not "the slightest probability that it will be adopted by the States."[26] The Report of the Joint Committee doubted that "the States would consent to surrender a power they had exercised, and to which they were attached," and therefore thought it best to "leave the whole question with the people of each State."[27] That such was the vastly preponderant opinion is confirmed by a remarkable fact: during the pendency of ratification of the amendment, Radical opposition to readmission of Tennessee because its constitution excluded Negro suffrage was voted down in the House by 125 to 12; and Senator Charles Sumner's parallel proposal was rejected by a 34 to 4 vote.[28] Finally, the provision for Negro suffrage in the Fifteenth Amendment testifies that it had been excluded from the Fourteenth, and so the framers of the Fifteenth said in unmistakable terms.[29] Let the whilom idol of the judicial activists, Justice Hugo Black, speak. He dismissed "rhapsodical strains about the duty of the Court to keep the Constitution in tune with the times." Instead, he said, "the idea is that the Constitution must be changed from time to time and that this Court is charged with the duty to make those changes. . . . The Constitution makers knew the need for change and provided for it by the amendment process of Article V."[30] Only the people, not the judges, are empowered to amend the Constitution.

The argument that reverse discrimination is required by the equal protection clause of the Fourteenth Amendment must begin with the question: what did the words mean to the framers who employed them? For this we look to their debates, for as Chief Justice Taney said, "The members of the Convention unquestionably used the words they inserted in the Constitution in the same sense in which they used them in their debates."[31] Senator Charles Sumner, the leading spokesman for Negro rights in the Thirty-ninth Congress, the Congress that framed the Fourteenth Amendment, expressed this sentiment unequivocally: "Every Constitution embodies the principles of its framers . . . If its meaning in any place is open to doubt, or if words are used which seem to have no fixed signification [e.g., equal protection], we cannot err if we turn to the framers."[32] Such sentiments were summarized in 1872 by "a unanimous Senate Judiciary Committee report, signed by Senators who had voted for the Thirteenth, Fourteenth, and Fifteenth Amendments in Congress."[33] The report stated, "A construction which would give the phrase . . . a meaning differing from the sense in which it was understood and employed by the people when they adopted the Constitution, would be as unconstitutional as a departure from the plain and express language of the Constitution in any other particular."[34] As Chief Justice Taney explained, "If . . . we are at liberty to give the old words new meanings when we find them in the Constitution, there is no power which may not, by this mode of construction, be conferred on the general government and denied to the States."[35] Chief Justice Marshall put it succinctly: The provisions of the Constitution are "not to be extended to objects . . . not contemplated by the framers."[36]

It is quite plain that the framers meant to exclude segregation from the scope of the amendment. Professor Nathaniel Nathanson of Northwestern University, himself an activist, wrote that Alexander Bickel "conclusively" proved that the amendment "would not require school desegregation" and that "Berger's independent research and analysis confirm and add weight to those conclusions."[37] Professor Henry Abraham of the University of Virginia considers that the framers "specifically rejected its [the Fourteenth Amendment] application to segregated schools."[38] There was first the fact, Bickel explained, that "It was preposterous to worry about unsegregated schools . . . when hardly a beginning had been made at educating Negroes at all and when obviously special efforts, suitable only for the Negroes, would have to be made."[39] James Wilson, chairman of the House Judiciary Committee and house manager of the Civil Rights Bill of 1866, which was considered to be "identical" to the Fourteenth Amendment and which the amendment was designed to "constitutionalize" and protect from repeal,[40] assured the framers that the bill did not require that black "children shall attend the same schools. These are not civil rights."[41] Initially the bill had contained a clause prohibiting "discrimination in civil rights";[42] that was deleted, stated Professor Alfred Kelly, a historian drawn into the desegregation case by the NAACP, "specifically to eliminate any reference to discriminatory practices like school segregation."[43] Congress, which had plenary control of the District of Columbia, repeatedly rejected efforts to bar segregated schools in the District.[44] How then can we attribute to Congress an intention to invade state sovereignty by providing for desegregation in the states? In fact, some thirteen Northern and Western states either provided for separate schools or excluded blacks altogether from public schools, and as Richard Kluger wrote, "If Congress and state legislatures had understood that the amendment was to wipe away the practices, surely there would have been more than a few howls."[45]

It is a cardinal mistake to read our own more generous sentiments into the minds of the framers. Whether it be a contract, will, or other document, the primary task of interpretation is to ascertain what was in the minds of the draftsmen.[46] Consider the climate in which they worked. An Indiana Radical, George Julian, lamented, "The real trouble is we hate the Negro."[47] Senator John Sherman of Ohio said in the Senate, "We do not like Negroes. We do not conceal our dislike."[48] There were a number of similar remarks,[49] epitomized by that of Senator Henry Wilson, a Radical from Massachusetts, in 1869: "There is not today a square mile in the United States, where the advocacy of equal rights and privileges of those colored men has not been in the past and is not now unpopular."[50]   The Senate gallery itself was segregated.[51]

One more example will suffice. When Congress, nine years after it had framed the Fourteenth Amendment, sought to broaden Negro rights, it refused to meddle with segregated schools. The Civil Rights Bill of 1875 initially placed equal access to the schools on the same footing with equal accommodations in inns, public conveyances and theaters. Despite Senator Sumner's strenuous endeavors, however, the school access provision was deleted. As Senator Aaron Sargent of California stated, the school proposal would reinforce "a prejudice powerful, permeating every part of the country, and existing more or less in every man's mind."[52] It needs to be emphasized that the Thirty-ninth Congress repeatedly rejected every attempt to prohibit all racial discrimination,[53] the reason, according to Senator William Fessenden of Maine, chairman of the Joint Committee on Reconstruction, being that, "We cannot put into the Constitution, owing to existing prejudices and existing institutions, an entire exclusion of all class distinctions."[54]

Whatever the framers' intention, the activists insist, it is overcome by the broad scope of the words "equal protection."[55] They would overturn a centuries-old canon of interpretation, reiterated by Judge Learned Hand, that the "manifest purpose overrides the text."[56] Moreover, those words are "inscrutable,"[57] according to Professor John Hart Ely, a perfervid admirer of Chief Justice Warren. Inscrutable words can hardly serve to curtail powers reserved to the states by the Tenth Amendment. That, Justice Miller declared, requires "language which expresses such a purpose too clearly to admit of doubt."[58] Men do not use words to defeat their own purposes. "We cannot rightly prefer" a meaning, said the Supreme Court, "which will defeat rather than effectuate the constitutional purpose."[59]   Then too, the debates show that the framers employed the words "equal protection" in a very limited context. At this point we must retrace our steps.

Having freed the slaves at the cost of a bitter war, the North found that the South sought by the Black Codes once more to reduce blacks to peonage and serfdom.[60] To protect the freedmen from a "damnable violence" and "fiendish oppression,"[61] the Civil Rights Bill of 1866 guaranteed the right to own property, to contract, and to have access to the courts.[62] These were the "fundamental rights" the framers meant to secure, no more.[63] As William Lawrence of Ohio stated, "It is a mockery to say that a citizen may have a right to live, and yet deny to him the right to make a contract to secure the privileges and rewards of labor."[64] In describing these aims the framers interchangeably referred to "equality," "equality before the law," and "equal protection," but always in the circumscribed context of the rights enumerated in the bill. Thus, Samuel Shellabarger of Ohio said, "Whatever rights as to each of these enumerated civil (not political) matters the State may confer upon one race . . . shall be held by all races in equality . . . . It secures . . . equality of protection in those enumerated rights."[65] In this way "equal protection" was given a special meaning in the Civil Rights Act of 1866; under a later Supreme Court decision the same meaning was to be given to those words in the related Fourteenth Amendment, which was enacted by the same Congress at the very same session.[66] A written constitution is subverted by a theory that leaves the justices free to jettison the meaning the framers attached to their words, as Madison and Chief Justice Taney had long since perceived.

Professor Kurland therefore stood on solid ground when he wrote that in the desegregation case, "the Court abandoned the search for the framers' intent . . . and chose instead to write a Constitution for our times."[67] Egalitarianism may be a worthy goal, but emphatically it was not that of the framers. "A belief in racial equality," wrote W. R. Brock, "was an abolitionist invention"; "to the majority of men in the midnineteenth century, it seemed to be condemned both by experience and by science."[68] A black professor, Dean Derrick Bell, has pointed out that "few abolitionists were interested in offering blacks the equality they touted so highly. Indeed the anguish most abolitionists experienced as to whether slaves should be granted social equality as well as political freedom is well documented."[69]

This is not to defend such sentiments but merely to emphasize that the words "equal protection," when employed by the framers, must be read in light of the framers' deep-seated prejudice against across-the-board equality. If those sentiments do not sit well with high-minded men today, the cure is not to credit the Court with power to read our meaning into words to which the framers gave a limited meaning, but to discard that limited meaning by means of an amendment. Nowhere have the people conferred upon the Court the power to amend the Constitution if they themselves have failed to do so.[70]

The founders adopted a written Constitution because they dreaded usurpation and sought to limit and diffuse the power they delegated.[71] They believed in a "fixed Constitution" with "bounds" no delegate

would "overleap," and they provided for future change by the process
of amendment submitted to the people.[72] Of the three branches, Hamilton assured the ratifiers, "the judiciary is next to nothing."[73] Judicial
review was an innovation, asserted in a few pre-1787 state cases proceeding for violation of express constitutional provisions, such as trial
by jury. None of these cases represented a takeover of legislative
policymaking, let alone constitutional revision. Even so, a few excited
stormy disapproval, leading to removal proceedings, because the
founders were attached to legislative paramountcy.[74]

The Constitution makes no specific provision for judicial review.
Learned Hand and Archibald Cox consider the evidence that the framers even contemplated judicial review to be inconclusive.[75] The argument for judicial review has largely rested on the framers' intention as
disclosed in the debates in the several Constitutional Conventions. If
we rely on the framers' intentions in establishing the power of judicial
review, we cannot disregard those same intentions in determining the
scope of that power. The current dismissal of the original intention,
and the dismissal of the meaning which the framers ascribed to the
terms they employed, would therefore undermine the legitimacy of judicial review itself. Judicial participation in legislative policymaking
was categorically rejected by the framers. It was proposed that the justices be members of a Council of Revision that would assist the President in exercising the veto power, on the ground that "laws may be
dangerous and unwise . . . and yet not so unconstitutional as to justify
judges in refusing to give them effect." But, Elbridge Gerry objected,
"it was quite foreign from the nature of ye office to make them judges of
the policy of public measures." Nathaniel Gorham chimed in that
judges "are not presumed to possess a peculiar knowledge of the mere
policy of public measures"; and Rufus King added that judges "ought
not to be legislators."[76] So judicial participation in legislative policymaking was rejected. Then too, as Gordon Wood found, the colonists
had "a profound fear of judicial . . . discretion,"[77] pungently expressed by Chief Justice Hutchinson of Massachusetts: "The Judges
should never be legislators. Because then the Will of the Judge would
be the law; and this tends to a state of slavery."[78]

Alexander Hamilton, the great proponent of judicial review, wrote
that courts may not "on the pretense of a repugnancy . . . substitute
their own pleasure to the constitutional intentions of the legislature."[79] That is, they may not intrude *within* the boundaries of legislative power. Their function was to make sure that those boundaries
were not "overleapt." Hamilton also assured the ratifiers that judges
would be impeached for "deliberate usurpations on the authority of the
legislature."[80]

In fine, we are dealing with a question of power: Who is to govern in our democracy, who is to make the policy choices for the nation—a group of unelected, unaccountable justices or the people themselves?[81] With Learned Hand I would maintain that "If we do need a third [legislative] chamber it should appear for what it is, not as the interpreter of inscrutable principles."[82] For one hundred years the "inscrutable" "equal protection" clause lay dormant, the last refuge of desperate counsel.[83] More recently, Professor Herbert Packer of Stanford University wrote, the clause "has under a different label permitted today's justices to impose their prejudices in much the same manner as the Four Horsemen once did,"[84] and with no more constitutional warrant. We cannot afford to condone a judicial decision, however desirable, that exercises a power which plainly was withheld. To do so is to undermine our democratic system. Disrespect for constitutional limitations, we learned from Watergate, breeds a Richard Nixon. Whether it be a Nixon or a Chief Justice Warren, we must insist on observance of constitutional limits.

NOTES

[1] Robert M. O'Neil, *Discriminating Against Discrimination: Preferential Admissions and the DeFunis Case* (Bloomington: Indiana University Press, 1975), p. 136.

[2] *New York Times* (February 20, 1981), p. B-1.

[3] O'Neil, op.cit., p. x.

[4] Ibid., p. 72.

[5] Letter to Harvard University Press (August 15, 1977).

[6] Paul Brest, "The Misconceived Quest for the Original Understanding," *Boston University Law Review*, 60(March 1980): 204, 236.

[7] Hearings on the Supreme Court before the Senate Subcommittee on Separation of Powers (90th Congress, 2nd Session, June 1968), p. 98.

[8] Excerpt from the autobiography of Justice William O. Douglas, *New York Times Magazine* (September 21, 1980), p. 40.

[9] Quoted in Raoul Berger, *Government by Judiciary: The Transformation of the Fourteenth Amendment* (Cambridge: Harvard University Press, 1977), p. 281; hereinafter "Berger, *G/J*." To reduce the volume of citations and direct attention to confirmatory materials, citations will be made to this book wherever possible.

[10] Ibid., p. 299.

[11] Activist professor Stanley Kutler wrote that "through the late 1930s, academic and liberal commentators . . . criticized vigorously the abusive

power of the federal judiciary [for] frustrating desirable social policies, [for] *arrogat[ing] a policy making function* not conferred upon them by the Constitution." Kutler, "Raoul Berger's Fourteenth Amendment: A History or A Historical?" *Hastings Constitutional Law Quarterly, 6* (Winter 1979): 511, 512-513, emphasis added.

[12] Long since, Chief Justice Marshall declared, "The peculiar circumstances of the moment may render a measure more or less wise, but cannot render it more or less constitutional," in G. Gunther, ed., *John Marshall's Defense of McCulloch v. Maryland* (Stanford, Cal.: Stanford University Press, 1969), pp. 190-191. "The criterion of constitutionality," said Justice Holmes, "is not whether we believe the law to be for the public good." *Adkins v. Children's Hospital*, 261 U.S. 525, 570 (1923), dissenting opinion.

[13] R. Berger, "Constructive Contempt: A Post Mortem," *University of Chicago Law Review*, 9 (June 1942): 602.

[14] Benjamin N. Cardozo, *The Nature of the Judicial Process* (New Haven: Yale University Press, 1921), pp. 129, 136.

[15] O'Neil, op. cit., pp. 91, 130.

[16] Ibid., pp. x, 38, 138.

[17] Professor Wallace Mendelson regards *Dred Scott* as a "disaster," that should "stand for all time as a warning to judges" against an "attempt to impose extra-constitutional policies upon the community under the guise of interpretation." Mendelson, "Raoul Berger's Fourteenth Amendment: Abuse by Contraction vs. Abuse by Expansion," *Hastings Constitutional Law Quarterly, 6* (Winter 1979): 437, 453.

[18] Quoted in Berger, G/J, pp. 117-118.

[19] *Griswold v. Connecticut*, 381 U.S. 473, 501 (1965), dissenting opinion.

[20] Louis Lusky, "'Government by Judiciary': What Price Legitimacy," *Hastings Constitutional Law Quarterly, 6* (Winter 1979): 403, 406.

[21] E.g., Henry J. Abraham, " 'Equal Justice Under Law' or 'Justice At Any Cost'? The Judicial Role Revisited: Reflections on Government By Judiciary: The Transformation of the Fourteenth Amendment," *Hastings Constitutional Law Quarterly, 6* (Winter 1979): 468, 469; Mendelson, op.cit., pp. 452, 453; Nathaniel L. Nathanson, "Constitutional Interpretation and the Democratic Process," *Texas Law Review*, 56(May-June 1978): 579, 581; see also R. Randall Bridwell, "Review of Berger's Government By Judiciary," *Duke Law Journal*, 1978(August 1978): 907, 911.

[22] Gerald Gunther, "Some Reflections on the Judicial Role: Distinctions, Roots, and Prospects," *Washington University Law Quarterly*, 1979(Summer 1979): pp. 817, 825.

[23] *Oregon v. Mitchell*, 400 U.S. 112, 256 (1970), dissenting in part.

[24] *Congressional Globe*, 39th Congress, 1st Session, 1866, p. 358.

[25] Ibid., p. 2766: "three fourths of the States of this Union could not be induced to vote to grant the right of suffrage."

[26] Ibid., p. 704.

[27] Berger, G/J, p. 84.

[28] Ibid., pp. 56, 59-60, 79.

[29] R. Berger, "The Fourteenth Amendment: Light from the Fifteenth," *Northwestern University Law Review*, 74(October 1979): 311, 321-22.

[30] *Griswold v. Connecticut*, 381 U.S. 479, 522 (1965), dissenting opinion.

[31] The Passenger Cases, 92 U.S. (7 How.) 283, 478 (1849), dissenting opinion; *Yates v. United States*, 354 U.S. 298, 319 (1957): "We should not assume that Congress . . . used the words 'advocate' and 'teach' in their ordinary dictionary sense when they had already been construed as terms of art carrying a special and limited connotation."

[32] *Congressional Globe*, op.cit., p. 677.

[33] Alfred Avins, ed., *The Reconstruction Amendments Debates: The Legislative History and Contemporary Debates in Congress on the Thirteenth, Fourteenth, and Fifteenth Amendments* (Richmond, Va.: Commission on Constitutional Government, 1967), p. ii.

[34] Ibid., pp. 571-572.

[35] The Passenger Cases, op.cit., dissenting opinion. Madison stated, if "the sense in which the Constitution was accepted and ratified by the Nations . . . be not the guide in expounding it, there can be no security . . . for a faithful exercise of its powers." Goullard Hunt, ed., *The Writings of James Madison* (New York: G. P. Putnam's Sons, 1900-10), 9: 191.

[36] *Ogden v. Saunders*, 25 U.S. (12 Wheat.) 213, 332 (1827), dissenting opinion.

[37] Nathanson, op. cit.

[38] Abraham, op. cit., p. 467.

[39] Berger, G/J, p. 100.

[40] Ibid., pp. 22-23.

[41] Ibid., p. 27.

[42] Ibid., p. 24.

[43] Ibid., p. 119. It was deleted at the insistence of Bingham, ibid., p. 120, the alleged conduit of abolitionist theology, ibid., pp. 119-120.

[44] Ibid., pp. 123-124.

[45] Ibid., p. 123.

[46] Stated by Thomas Rutherforth, published in 1756, a "work well known to the colonists," ibid., p. 366, and which Justice Story commended as a guide to constitutional construction. For this and similar citations, see R. Berger, " 'Government by Judiciary': Judge Gibbons Argument Ad Hominem," *Boston University Law Review*, 59(July 1979): 783, 805. "Of course," Justice Holmes wrote, "the purpose of written instruments is to express some intention or state of mind of those who write them, and it is desirable to make this purpose effective." Oliver Wendell Holmes, *Collected Legal Papers* (New York: Harcourt, Brace, and Howe, 1920), p. 206.

[47] Berger, *G/J*, p. 91.

[48] Ibid., p. 233.

[49] Ibid., p. 13.

[50] Ibid., p. 240.

[51] Ibid., p. 125.

[52] Berger, "The Fourteenth Amendment," op. cit., p. 329.

[53] Berger, *G/J*, pp. 163-164.

[54] Ibid., p. 99.

[55] E.g., Professor John Hart Ely maintains that the framers issued an "open and across-the-board invitation to import into the constitutional decision process considerations that will not be found in the amendment." Ely, "Constitutional Interpretivism: Its Allure and Impossibility," *Indiana Law Journal*, 53(Spring 1978): 399, 415. For comment thereon, see R. Berger, "'Government by Judiciary: John Hart Ely's 'Invitation'," *Indiana Law Journal*, 54(Winter 1979): p. 277.

[56] *Cawley v. United States*, 272 F.2d 443, 445 (2d Cir. 1959); *Hawaii v. Mankichi*, 190 U.S. 197, 212 (1903).

[57] Ely states that the "privileges or immunities" clause is "quite inscrutable," and that the "Equal Protection Clause" is "equally unforthcoming with details." J. Ely, *Democracy and Distrust: A Theory of Judicial Review* (Cambridge: Harvard University Press, 1980), p. 98.

[58] Slaughterhouse Cases, 83 U.S. (16 Wall.) 26, 78 (1872).

[59] *United States v. Classic*, 313 U.S. 299, 316 (1941).

[60] Berger, *G/J*, pp. 26-27.

[61] Ibid.

[62] Ibid., p. 24.

[63] Senator William Stewart of Nevada explained that the purpose of the Civil Rights Bill "is simply to remove the disabilities existing by laws tending to reduce the negro to a system of peonage. It strikes at that; nothing else." *Congressional Globe*, op. cit., p. 1785. In a discussion of the Fourteenth Amendment, for which he voted, James W. Patterson of New Hampshire said he was opposed "to any law discriminating against [blacks] in the security of life, liberty, person and property . . . Beyond this I am not prepared to go." Ibid., p. 2699.

[64] Ibid., p. 1833.

[65] Berger, *G/J*, pp. 169-170. Leonard Myers of Pennsylvania said that each state should be required to provide "equal protection of life, liberty, and property, equal rights to sue and be sued, make contracts, and give testimony," rights theretofore denied to blacks. *Congressional Globe*, op.cit., p. 1622.

[66] *Reiche v. Smythe*, 80 U.S. (13 Wall.) 162, 165 (1871); see also *Yates v. United States*, op. cit.

[67] Philip B. Kurland, " 'Brown v. Board of Education Was the Beginning' The School Desegregation Cases in the United States Supreme Court: 1954-1979," *Washington University Law Quarterly*, 1979(Spring 1979): 309, 313.

[68] Berger, *G/J*, p. 13.

[69] Ibid., p. 167. Professor David Donald wrote that the suggestion that "Negroes should be treated as equals to white men woke some of the deepest and ugliest fears in the American mind." Ibid., p. 12.

[70] Justice Harlan declared, "When the Court disregards the express intent and understanding of the Framers, it has invaded the realm of the political process to which the amending power was committed, and it has violated the constitutional structure which it is its highest duty to protect." *Oregon v. Mitchell*, 400 U.S. 112, 202-203 (1970), dissenting opinion.

[71] R. Berger, *Congress v. the Supreme Court* (Cambridge: Harvard University Press, 1969), pp. 12-16.

[72] Justice William Paterson, who had been one of the most influential framers, declared that "The Constitution is certain and fixed; it contains the permanent will of the people . . . and can be revoked or altered only by the authority that made it." Van Horne's Lessee v. Dorrance, 2 U.S. (2 Dall.) 304, 308 (C.C.Pa. 1795); P. Kurland, *Watergate and the Constitution* (Chicago: University of Chicago Press, 1978), p. 7.

[73] *The Federalist*, No. 78 (New York: Modern Library Edition, 1937), p. 504.

[74] Berger, *Congress v. the Supreme Court*, op. cit., pp. 36-42.

[75] See R. Berger, "The Scope of Judicial Review: An Ongoing Debate," *Hastings Constitutional Law Quarterly*, 1979(Winter 1979): 536.

[76] R. Berger, " 'The Supreme Court as a Legislature': A Dissent," *Cornell Law Review*, 64(August 1979): 988, 994-996.

[77] Gordon Wood, *The Creation of the American Republic, 1776-1787* (Chapel Hill: University of North Carolina Press, 1969), p. 296.

[78] Berger, *G/J*, p. 307.

[79] *The Federalist*, No. 80, op. cit., p. 507.

[80] Ibid., No. 81, pp. 526-527.

[81] The distinguished legal historian, Professor Willard Hurst of the University of Wisconsin, perceived in 1954 that "the real issue is who is to make the policy choices in the twentieth century: judges or the combination of legislature and electorate that makes constitutional amendments?" Berger, *G/J*, p. 315.

[82] Ibid., p. 46.

[83] *Buck v. Bell*, 274 U.S. 200, 208 (1926).

[84] Berger, *G/J*, pp. 191-192.

ETHNICITY AND THE LAW: OF POLICY AND THE CONSTITUTION

Robert M. O'Neil

President, University of Wisconsin System

These are hard times for affirmative action. That much became clear a few days after the 1980 election, when Senator Orrin G. Hatch proclaimed to the press, "I will outlaw affirmative action." Apart from its curiously personalized view of the legislative process, this statement was startling for its substance. While many doubts remain about the degree to which affirmative action is required or even permitted as a matter of constitutional law, supporters and critics alike would concede the difficulty of ending overnight a governmental policy which has been two decades in development. Yet that is apparently what Senator Hatch vowed in November 1980, and what he has continued to seek. Senator Hatch is not alone—nor is his the first such challenge. Representative Robert Walker of Pennsylvania introduced a somewhat milder bill that would, by amending the 1964 Civil Rights Act, forbid racial quotas in college and university admissions policies and employment. There has been also a nearly successful and persistent effort to restrict the jurisdiction of the federal courts in school desegregation cases. Glancing blows at affirmative action programs, including the numerous so-called "reverse discrimination" suits, have been a fact of life for much of the past decade. Yet the intensity and apparent breadth of support for the Hatch Amendment may mark a new era.

In opening Senate subcommittee hearings on affirmative action, Senator Hatch characterized affirmative action as "a medieval notion of government by status" which seemed to him wholly at variance with the principles of civil rights. He has introduced a constitutional amendment which would, at the very least, forbid race-conscious preferential programs of the kind that have been sustained by many courts during the past ten years. A central premise of the amendment is that legislative and administrative action favoring or protecting minorities in employment, education, and other sectors violates the spirit of the Constitution. Any doubts about the intent or the current meaning of the equal protection clause of the Fourteenth Amendment should be put to rest through the process of further amendment. The courts should, Senator Hatch urges, be told in no uncertain terms that they may neither compel nor condone race-conscious preferential programs or policies.

We cannot now revisit the basic issue in all its dimensions, and should avoid the very complex issues of affirmative action in employment. It should be noted, though, if only in passing, that most steps which have been taken—in both the public and the private sectors— have been designed to implement Title VII of the 1964 Civil Rights Act. It would be easy enough to repeal or modify Title VII (or any other part of the 1964 law) without a constitutional amendment. It would also be quite possible to nullify by statute the force of such administrative edicts as Executive Order 11246. We shall, however, resist the temptation to say more about employment and other programs and concentrate instead on higher education.

In trying to determine what it is Senator Hatch wants to outlaw in higher education, we should recognize how relatively modest is the current scope of the law. We must for that purpose go back a bit more than a decade—a brief refresher course for those who may have forgotten the history, or may even have come in relatively late in the drama. The very first preferential admission case reached the Supreme Court in 1970. It was the fascinating suit brought by Marco DeFunis, Jr., against the University of Washington and its law school. This was originally not a challenge to the minority portion of the program, but rather a plea for a preference based on geography since DeFunis was a Washington resident and taxpayer aggrieved by the admission of non-residents to the increasingly selective professional graduate programs. The Washington Supreme Court held against DeFunis, after finding that the university and the law school had a compelling interest in considering race as a factor in the admission process. That remains one of the very few such decisions. The United States Supreme Court agreed to review the case, but then ducked the issue when it appeared that DeFunis was in his final semester and would graduate regardless of which way the Court held. That declaration of mootness suggests a quality of adjudication to which I would like to make passing reference, since it touches on Professor Berger's preceding chapter. On numerous occasions, going back to the 1957 refusal to reach the merits of a challenge to Virginia's miscegenation law, through the deference given to Congress on the public accommodation issue during the sit-in case period, to the refusal to decide the merits of the Los Angeles county employment case just three years ago, there seems to be a marked reluctance to reach the merits of these thorny issues sooner or

more broadly than necessary. This is, however, a side issue which we
will not consider further here.

The non-decision in *DeFunis* left the field open. During the ensuing
years there were several inconclusive cases, most of which foundered on
the "standing" issue, typically holding that even if the preferential
programs were legally vulnerable, a particular non-minority plaintiff
would not prevail because no court could tell whether he or she would
be the first to be admitted if the program did not exist. That may all
sound rather evasive to non-lawyers, but it did tend to slow the development of the law in the post-*DeFunis* period. There were two notable
cases during this era—one holding that Georgetown University violated Title VI by reserving a very large share of its financial aid for a
small group of minority students, drawing the line solely on the basis of
race; the other that the City College of New York acted unconstitu-
tionally in admitting the last eight students to its new biomedical program on strictly racial criteria. Neither case received much attention in
the press even though in the City College case the judge held that university officials might be liable for civil damages to applicants who had
been unlawfully excluded from the program. The case was eventually
settled, but the threat of personal liability continues to hang over the
heads of anyone who administers a legally vulnerable race-conscious
program.

Those were about the only significant decisions in the period between *DeFunis* and *Bakke*. In *Bakke*, of course, the California Supreme
Court held that the Davis Medical School had improperly reserved sixteen places in its entering class for minorities, since that group was admitted through a separate process and the places for them were set
aside solely on the basis of race. That case was the vehicle to return the
whole matter to the U.S. Supreme Court, which split in three diverse
directions in the summer of 1978. Let me recapitulate briefly, and then
offer a few observations on the rather limited focus of *Bakke*. There was
no clear opinion for the Court. Four justices would have upheld the
Davis program, despite the claim that it involved a racial "quota" and
did select applicants on the basis of race. Four others would have inval-
idated it on quite narrow grounds, reserving the constitutional issue for
a later case in which it was better presented and had to be judged. (For
them the California program was vulnerable under Title VI of the 1964
Civil Rights Act, and that was enough.) The ninth member of the
Court, Justice Powell, split the issues and went with one group on the
broader issue, and with the other on the validity of the Davis program.
Thus there were five votes for the general proposition that race might
be taken into account in admissions programs—under certain conditions which emerged alone in Powell's opinion; and five votes for the

holding that the Davis program did not meet those conditions. Despite all the furor which the case aroused, it should be clear that it actually held somewhat less than either its critics or its supporters claimed for it at the time.

Let us consider the modest nature of *Bakke*, because any assessment of what Senator Hatch intends requires such a context. First, no member of the Court foreclosed the use of race in determining who should receive higher education. Five justices clearly held that the California Supreme Court erred in forbidding race-conscious admissions policies. The other four justices did not speak to the issue and, indeed, warned those who might be tempted to find in their opinion any indication of a broader judgment not to do so. They expressly reserved the constitutional issue of the role of race for a later case and addressed only the legality of the single admissions program before the Court. It is most significant that no justice disapproved the use of race on constitutional grounds.

Second, at least five justices presumably would sustain some type of race-conscious admissions program, such as the Harvard College program to which Justice Powell referred with clear approval. There is, however, a hint that Justices Brennan, White, Marshall and Blackmun would require some showing of past discrimination against the groups favored by such a program, and would need to be convinced that such a program would not stigmatize those groups. Curiously, Justice Powell may have been more ready to uphold certain race-conscious programs than were the four other justices who approved even the Davis program. An obvious warning emerges: In designing any race-conscious policy to capture a majority of the present Court, one must be careful not to lose any of the Brennan group in the course of seeking Justice Powell's approval.

Third, a bare majority of the Court did strike down the Davis admissions program, although on different grounds. It is uncertain what factual variations might shift the vote of one member of that tenuous majority. Simply altering the number of places reserved for minority applicants from sixteen to fifteen or seventeen obviously would not alter the result, but relatively subtle changes in the process by which applications were reviewed, or in the resulting minority representation, could well produce a different alignment.

In extrapolating from these propositions, we must be mindful of the peculiar factual context of the *Bakke* case. Neither the Harvard nor the Davis program is representative of the spectrum of admissions policies used today by institutions of higher education. The Davis program was extraordinary in the high degree to which it employed race as a criterion of admission. The Harvard program is quite distinctive in other ways. While many institutions of higher learning must be selective, their applicant pools seldom contain the richness and variety of the group of high school seniors who seek admission to Harvard College. The simple fact is that most admissions policies are quite unlike either the Harvard or the Davis program, and their validity thus must be judged by analogy.

What has happened since *Bakke* reinforces my comments about its limited nature. There have been a few more procedurally inconclusive skirmishes, and one that did reach the merits. The case on the merits comes, curiously, from the law school of the University of California at Davis. A former dean of the law school at Berkeley, Frank Newman, was ready and waiting for the case in his new capacity as a justice of the California Supreme Court, along with some other post-*Bakke* appointees.

The California Court of Appeal had held that the Davis law school minority program foundered on the *Bakke* principles, and that was the end of the matter. (I might add as a curious footnote that one will never find that opinion if one now looks for it; California has a unique practice of washing out the intermediate appellate opinion when the Supreme Court agrees to review a case, and thus the decision along the way is treated as though it never existed.) The California Supreme Court held by a substantial 5-2 margin that the Davis law program was distinguishable from the Davis medical program because it took many factors into account, reviewed applicants as individuals, and did not set aside a specific number of "minority" slots as the medical program had done. The court found a close correspondence to the Harvard program which had so appealed to Justice Powell in *Bakke,* as did the majority opinion in the more recent *DeRonde* case, decided in February 1981:

> The admissions procedures in this case do not vary in any significant way from the Harvard program. Minority racial or ethnic origin was one of several competing factors used by the law school to reach its ultimate decision of whether or not to admit a particular applicant. As Justice Powell pointedly observed, the primary and obvious defect in the *Bakke* quota system was that it precluded individualized consideration of every applicant without regard to race. That fatal flaw does not appear in the admissions procedures before this court; this is not a quota case.
>
> Justice Brennan, representing the views of four justices, would have upheld the quota system invalidated by the majority in *Bakke.* It may fairly be concluded that a race-conscious law school admissions program that does not involve a quota, *a fortiori,* would be sustained by those holding the Brennan view. Justice Brennan would hold that even a racial quota system such as involved in *Bakke* is constitutional if its purpose is to remove the

disparate racial impact a school's actions might otherwise have and if there is reason to believe that the disparate impact is itself the product of past discrimination, whether its own or that of society at large.

Here, the evidence supports a finding that the use of a race-conscious admissions program was needed to prevent a disproportionate underrepresentation of minorities in the school. Further, past societal discrimination against ethnic minorities is an unfortunate, but demonstrable, historical fact acknowledged in both the Powell and Brennan opinions in *Bakke*.

There was one other factor in the California high court. One year before this decision, a majority of that court had upheld an employment program which involved a quota-like racial preference, finding that *Bakke* did not preclude such a holding. Now the California court carried that analysis back into higher education and in *DeRonde* sustained a program which—despite the obvious factual differences from the Davis medical program—probably would not have passed muster with that court earlier.

That completes the report on the current state of the law. What does it suggest? I would draw several inferences. For one, the few courts that have sustained—actually validated—preferential programs on the merits have done so cautiously and with qualifications. In both the Washington Supreme Court *DeFunis* decision and the California court's *DeRonde*—and also in a New York Court of Appeals case under the name of *Alevy*, which was pre-*DeFunis*—the scope of the holding is quite narrow. Second, it is obvious but worth noting that such cases involve only the question whether colleges and universities *may* take race into account, and not whether they *must* do so. (The employment area remains quite different; we are talking here only about higher education.) Third, the programs that have been sustained could not reasonably be regarded as having racial quotas, since the numbers vary from year to year and applicants are considered as individuals rather than simply as members of racial or ethnic groups. Finally, the courts have consistently required some clear declaration of either state or university policy, or both, as a basis for validating such preferential programs.

One might plead that we miss the forest for the trees in discussing such seemingly technical and legal aspects of this highly complex and often emotional issue. A detailed summary of the underlying rationale of race-conscious programs would demonstrate the kind of case which Justice Powell saw as constitutionally compelling in his *Bakke* opinion. Even without such a summary, however, we can be assured of the appropriateness of certain observations about these programs. Surely the quest for diversity is a legally significant consideration; if higher education has one relevant mission, it is to expose students to a broad and reasonably representative cross section of society and the American population. Surely the historic underrepresentation of minority and disadvantaged groups for reasons that are not of their own making, including the effects of standardized tests, is also important. There is, too, the special value of better serving underserved communities—a factor which Justice Powell thought might be legally valid if it had been better demonstrated than the University of California was able to do in its *Bakke* brief. Finally, the actual results may be notable. During the last decade the number of minority students has substantially increased at all levels. Not so long ago we realized there were more black students then enrolled in accredited law schools across the country than the number of black attorneys admitted to practice in all states. The number of black students enrolled in colleges across the nation has doubled since 1970, and since 1976 blacks have been represented in colleges at about the same proportion as in the national population of college-age persons. (Of course, that figure is buoyed by the still substantial enrollments in the predominantly black colleges, and the situation is far less encouraging for other minorities than for blacks.) In short, taking higher education as one relevant measure, very substantial progress has occurred since the time a decade ago when we began to worry acutely and take steps to remedy the imbalance in our enrollments.

Two final questions might be posed. One has to do with the effect of racially preferential programs on non-minorities; is there evidence that non-minority students and applicants, and the groups from which they come, have been harmed as a result of these programs? Arguably, as with Amitai Etzioni's studies of the open admissions program at the City University of New York, non-minority persons from socio-economically disadvantaged groups have benefited rather than suffered by reason of the emphasis on minority access. Even in highly selective professional programs, there is no hard evidence that persons of Eastern and Southern European ancestry are today less well represented in higher education than they were a decade ago, as many feared when race-conscious programs were instituted.

Finally, we might ask what would happen if in fact the Hatch Amendment did become a part of our Constitution. It is nice to believe that we have made enough progress so that even the prohibition of race-preferential programs, at least in public higher education, would not bring disaster. This is not to suggest that the Hatch Amendment and other like proposals should not be vigorously opposed, but it is likely that the harm would be more psychological than practical, and that much of the gain that has been made during the past decade could survive even so basic a change in the law. More should we fear the gravest consequences for the feelings and perceptions of minorities— and for those in the non-minority community who have been deeply committed to expanding opportunity in higher education and other sectors of national life. A declaration by the requisite share of the American people that race may never be considered, even to correct the effects of past discrimination, would be a profoundly disturbing development. We hope it will not come to pass, but these are indeed very hard times for affirmative action. Let us hope that things will look a bit brighter in the future.

THE SCHOOL AND THE JUDGE

Nathan Glazer

Harvard University

Two contradictions leap out when one considers the ten-year history of intervention by the legal process into how the educational process deals with race and ethnicity. The first is a contradiction between the two great objectives of this intervention. One great objective, of course, has been to overcome the segregation of blacks, and in a much lesser degree other groups, into separate schools in the public school system. The other great objective has been to define and prescribe educational programs suitable for children of non-English speaking families, overwhelmingly Spanish speakers of Mexican and Puerto Rican origin.

The contradiction between these two great objectives of legal intervention is not necessarily direct though on occasion it is: when, for example, a policy adopted by a court requires the distribution of black and Hispanic children evenly throughout the school system and classes, while at the same time, a distinctive curriculum mandated for the Spanish-speaking requires some degree of concentration. This does happen, and is a source of difficulty in some school systems undergoing desegregation; but the contradictions I have in mind lie deeper than this somewhat technical procedure, and would exist even when there are so many children of Spanish background (as in Los Angeles) that an even distribution throughout the system would always provide enough Spanish-speaking students to enable the school to form classes of these children for distinctive educational objectives. The deeper contradiction I will try to develop is between a school system that tries to treat its children under a cloak of ignorance about race and ethnic background, and one that specifically aims at treating its children in the light of, and under the influence of, their race and ethnic background.

This fundamental contradiction in how we see the function of the public schools in a multi-racial and multi-ethnic society demands far more examination than it has yet received, and we must be grateful to the judicial process for bringing this contradiction sharply to our attention. We can, alas, rarely count on the legislative process to do so; legislators deal with general principles rather than specific cases, and have often been content to pronounce two general principles as matters of law, even when they are in potential or actual contradiction, leaving it to administrators and judges to try to sort out which shall prevail in any given case, or what balance shall be set between them.

Before entering on this examination, however, let me record the second contradiction, one which has recently come to our attention and will, I believe, dominate legal arguments over schooling in the 1980s: This is the contradiction between what judges have been prescribing for school systems in the wake of interpretations of the Constitution and federal law deeply influenced by advocates putting themselves forward as representatives of black, Hispanic and other minority students, and what present-day scholarship suggests is effective for education. What the advocates have been demanding, and the judges prescribing, almost ensures, in the light of our current research, that we will face some drag on the effectiveness of education. This is a serious matter indeed, and it is only in the past few years that research has made it possible to raise the issue sharply.

Let us initially, however, consider the first contradiction between the needs of black children for desegregation and the needs of limited English-speaking ability students for special programs, as they both have been shaped by court decisions, Congressional legislation and administrative interpretation. If "desegregation" had retained the meaning that seemed integral to it for the first fifteen years after the *Brown* decision, the contradiction would not arise. Its initial meaning appeared to be the elimination of state and local requirements for the separation of children in schools by race. That was the specific legislation attacked; what was intended in that attack was nothing more than its replacement by a racially neutral pattern of assignment, and since that was then almost universally assignment on the basis of residence, it seemed the obvious approach to desegregation. Indeed, in 1954 it was the most sweeping approach to desegregation envisaged, one which the Deep South states tried to avoid and the border states almost immediately adopted. The model, ironic as it now seems, was the North and West where, whatever the pattern of state and local segregation in the past, and sometimes the relatively recent past, the fact was that students attended schools on the basis of where they lived. If desegregation had retained that original meaning and had been considered satisfied by a racially neutral means of assignment, no conflict between desegregation and bilingual education would have arisen. High concentrations of black students would have undoubtedly remained in many schools, but there also would have been concentrations of Spanish-speaking children, or children of other foreign language background, in

other schools. The need of bilingual education for some degree of concentration of its recipients would have been met, and at least this first
contradiction would not have arisen on a practical level. As we know,
however, the operative meaning of desegregation changed in 1971 in
the *Swann* case. Whatever the pious disclaimers of the Supreme Court
that it is not aiming at racial balance, the only desegregation remedy
within a school district that is sure of acceptance by the Court—the
model which desegregation plaintiffs try to reach, and often do—is a
pattern of assignment of students to schools by race so that each school
approximates closely the distribution of plaintiff-class children in the
school district as a whole. This is what happened in Charlotte-Meck-
lenburg, in San Francisco, in Denver, in Boston, in Cleveland, in Dayton and Columbus, and in many other jurisdictions. It is true some
school districts have as yet escaped such a universal scheme because
school authorities, with more or less agreement from plaintiffs, have
implemented some lesser degree of even distribution (through magnet
programs, busing to special programs for only part of the school day or
week, and the like), or because even the plaintiffs falter before a universal application of this approach in a school district the size of New
York City; but if this pattern of even assignment by race has been
fought for so vigorously in a school district as large in numbers and
geography as Los Angeles, one suspects New York is not far behind.

It is even distribution, not desegregation in the sense in which it was
originally understood, that creates the problem of contradiction. And
it is the right to even distribution, or in a word—dispersion, that blacks
have gained. But if blacks have the right to even distribution—a right,
be it noted, that when once granted must be accepted by the grateful
beneficiaries even if they have considerable doubt as to its value, as
many black parents do—what about other minorities? Our jurisprudence is burdened with the problem of "equal protection," and does
not define any specific minority as being uniquely entitled to "equal
protection." The Fourteenth Amendment was undoubtedly passed for
the benefit of the freed slaves, all black, but its protections have been
applied to other ethnic and racial groups; few object, because it was
phrased in universalistic and all-embracing terms, and this extension
by the Supreme Court of the intention of Congress and the states that
endorsed it, if not other extensions, does gain general approval. If the
blacks are entitled to the right of dispersal, and in fact to its requirement, are not other minorities equally so entitled? But suppose they
have other pressing interests, and do not find the right one they wish to
invoke or enjoy?

The problem might not have arisen in the context of the Southeast,
where white and black form almost the entire population, and there are

few intermediate groups to confuse the picture. (Even in the Deep South, however, there are Indians and Asians and others to complicate the sharp black-white division.) This is not the case, though, in the rest of the country. We have large Spanish-speaking populations, or ethnic groups descended from Spanish-speaking immigrants, who are quite diverse in their degree of assimilation and acculturation, their characteristic level of achievement in school, and the extent of their integration into political and economic life. Among Cubans in Miami, Puerto Ricans in Boston, Mexican Americans in Texas and California, Colombians in New York, Nicaraguans in San Francisco, and a not insubstantial number of people who actually did come from Spain as immigrants, and their descendants, there is little in common. All are now considered "Hispanic Americans," and a judge in a desegregation suit is faced with the problem: What should he or she do about them? Treat them as whites, as was naively or maliciously done in some early desegregation plans, so that a majority Mexican American school with no Anglos and a minority of blacks could be considered desegregated? Consider them as having the same status as blacks, equally entitled to dispersion? Consider them to have special rights that the desegregation plan must reflect? And however they are considered, what is their legal status in a desegregation suit? The plaintiff represents only the black children, and while there may be intervenors for the Spanish-speaking in many desegregation cases, just what the rights of the Spanish-speaking should be, and whether they should be allowed to appear at the liability phase (which may well determine the nature of the remedy), or only at the remedy stage, and just what degree of claim they have in shaping the decree, are knotty matters.

Some elements in the Hispanic American population—Puerto Ricans and Mexican Americans—have the best claim of putting themselves in the posture of black plaintiffs as an aggrieved minority subject to discrimination and segregation (though their situation is by no means identical to that of blacks). To confuse matters, others such as Cubans have been a benefited minority—assisted in migrating and in obtaining jobs and housing. Still others, such as the current migrants from the Caribbean, Central America and South America, are akin to older immigrants of the age of mass immigration—neither assisted nor facing any particular discrimination, coming to the United States out of the desire to escape poverty or political disorder or discrimination, and hoping to find educational and economic advancement. How do they fit into the problem? Should they be likened in law to the white? The black? Made a special category? Finally, there are increasing numbers of Asians, a term which includes Japanese, Chinese, Filipinos, Koreans, Asian Indians, Vietnamese, Cambodians and Laotians—of whom all groups but the first are increasing rapidly. In the large cities the numbers of children of such groups in the public schools are becoming substantial. In the late 1960s and early 1970s, affirmative action programs assigned the Chinese and Japanese the status of minorities that have faced discrimination and deserve redress. Unfortunately, the general term "Asian American" was applied to them; it now seems to cover all the others, who may thereby gain rights that seem somewhat greater than those held by other Americans of non-Asian and non-Hispanic background, and who are neither American Indian nor black.

Thus there are complexities in dealing with the status of Hispanic Americans and Asians and American Indians in desegregation suits. They were perhaps first faced in the school desegregation suit in San Francisco, a city in which blacks were a minority of the public school population—but then so were the Hispanics, the Asians and the whites. What emerged from that suit was a plan for four-fold even distribution—blacks, Chinese, whites and Hispanics were all required to accept the right of even distribution. The latter three resisted.

Up to this point in the story, we have a right, beginning as one to desegregation and ending as one to dispersion, now being imposed not only on blacks and whites, but on Hispanics and Asians as well. But what can stand before a right? Only another right. The desire of the non-black groups to be undisturbed in their enjoyment of their neighborhood schools was not recognized as such a right. Thus the right to dispersion carried all before it. But now another largely judicially created right rose up to challenge the first judicially created right to dispersion: It was a right to bilingual education, and thus a right, in effect, to some degree of concentration. This is a dilemma that has faced many judges dealing with desegregation suits. How can the opportunity for bilingual education, as it is called, be protected in the face of the right to dispersion?[1]

Bilingual education now requires a definition. On occasion it is someone teaching a class in two languages, but it generally means one teacher teaching the class in a non-English language and another teaching the class in English. The pertinent legislation, state and federal, which either provides funds for it (federal) or mandates it under certain circumstances (state), envisages bilingual education as a temporary educational effort to adapt children to the English-speaking school. The proponents of bilingual education, however, see it as a mechanism to maintain competence in the native language, and would like to see such maintenance a regular obligation of the school. This is generally summarized as the conflict between "transitional" and "maintenance" bilingual education. The first generally has the support of elected officials; the second has the support generally of bilingual administrators and teachers. Whatever the legislation and the regulations, where ethnic group pressures are strong, bilingual education becomes maintenance-of-foreign language-and-culture education. Thus, the education of Spanish-speaking children in New York City, regulated by the *Aspira* consent decree, the largest program of bilingual education in the country, consists basically of education for most of the school day in all academic subjects in Spanish, with one class of English, and with mixed classes for physical education, art, shop and the like. There is no regular mechanism for transfer out of the Spanish-language program, and students, it appears, will spend most of their time in the New York City schools through high school in such a program, unless their parents make an effort—which they are allowed under the decree—to get them out.[2] With such an approach to education, and when such an education becomes a right—as it has in the *Aspira* consent judgment and in other legal actions—the conflict with the right to dispersion can be severe.

"Bilingual programs, to maintain any semblance of quality in the real world, need to meet a critical mass threshold,"[3] we are told by Bruce Cohen, a lawyer trying to reconcile these rights. They need enough students so that students of different ages and learning needs and abilities need not be accommodated willy-nilly in the same class. A program, according to its proponents, must span several consecutive grades—three years is considered a minimum. Then, there are shortages of skilled bilingual teachers, and they cannot be spread too thin. And would one or two teachers in a school be enough for a program? Similarly with administrators. Programs desirably should be varied and experimental, since we do not know the best approach, and thus one needs a center for monitoring and analysis, preferably in a school where a number of programs are being carried out. "So much effort," Cohen concludes, "has gone into challenging the dual school system that it is difficult to step back and separate the easily applied numerical standard from the underlying qualitative objective."[4]

Some judges, we are told, have failed to consider the needs of the Spanish-speaking for bilingual education. The Tenth Circuit, overruling the exclusion of some schools with model bilingual and bicultural programs and large Chicano populations from the Denver desegregation requirements, asserted:

Bilingual education . . . is not a substitute for desegregation. Although bilingual instruction may be required to prevent the isolation of minority students in a predominantly Anglo school system . . . such instruction must be subordinate to a plan of school desegregation.[5] We therefore remand this portion of the case for a determination whether the continued segregation of students at

the five mentioned schools may be justified on grounds other than
the institution and development of bilingual-bicultural programs
at the schools.[6]

Bruce Cohen and, in another article, Peter D. Roos, argue that there
is no need for such a conflict, and that the needs of both groups can be
accommodated. They give the example of a number of desegregation
decrees where this has been done. But the contortions necessary to produce this accommodation are wondrous to behold, even if the advocates of both bilingual education and segregation find them satisfactory. Thus, Roos, Director for Educational Litigation of the Mexican
American Legal Defense Fund, describes approvingly the "model" arrangements in the Boston desegregation case:

> The decree ordered the assignment of LESA [Limited English-
> Speaking Ability] students before others, to prevent their disper-
> sal. The court resolved the problem by initially concluding that
> three consecutive bilingual classes were the minimum necessary
> for an effective program of bilingual instruction, which would
> mean an enrollment of sixty LESA students—twenty students
> each grade level. Then the court determined how large the minor-
> ity population in each school should be. For example, a previ-
> ously all-white school might be required to have a student body
> that was 40 per cent minority . . . . If the sixty LESA students
> brought the minority percentage of that school to 20 per cent,
> then the remaining 20 per cent of the minority students would be
> black. Thus, LESA students first had to be identified, the mini-
> mally acceptable number of such students for effective bilingual
> instruction had to be determined, and finally, only after LESA
> students were assigned would the other minority students and the
> Anglo students be assigned. [Footnotes omitted.][7]

That program may satisfy the advocates of the Mexican American
Legal Defense Fund, but suppose there are also students in need of
Chinese, or French Creole, education, a not unlikely situation in inner-
city Boston? In the average Boston school, which is small, there would
scarcely be room for a properly desegregating number of black and
white children. Or perhaps one or another of the bilingual programs
would have to be moved, only because there was no room for both the
program and the other categories of children necessary to desegregate
the school (not that in many programs there would, in any case, be
much interaction between them). This is not an unlikely development,
for as we find on reading further in Bruce Cohen's article, he is not so
happy with Judge Garrity's perspicacity. Hispanic intervenors in Boston sought a plan that would retain clusters both for ongoing programs
and those not implemented. Two problems in making the plan, however, were that not all Hispanic children needed bilingual classes, and

many who did were not in school. The intervenors sought an order that would require the school committee to "locate, screen, and classify such students." The court accepted the need for clustering, and provided sites for bilingual programs. But when the court adopted Phase III of the reassignment plan, it "inexplicably . . . 'decimated' half the clustered sites established two years earlier." The Hispanic intervenors immediately requested the court to withdraw approval of the new plan, but the judge refused. Conceivably, there were so many factors to be accommodated in the assignment plan that the judge simply decided to ignore the interests of one group.

There was another misunderstanding over the order to require the school district to "locate, screen, and classify" students. "For no apparent reason . . . . the explicit order to the school district limited the scope of the census to those children out of school." Perhaps the judge was so influenced by the concern of the Hispanic-group intervenors for the children out of school that he forgot those in school. In any case, this order, issued February 25, 1975, was not expanded to include children in school until May 6, 1977. Even then the intervenors were not happy: "[T]here has yet to issue an explicit order that the School Committee 'identify' by its own efforts Spanish-speaking children. At the present time, it appears that parents must apply to have their children screened for eligibility for programs."[8]

Admittedly, it is easy hunting for a critic of both the new right to dispersion and the administratively and judicially required right to a certain kind of bilingual-bicultural education, as well as of judicial interventionism, to find contradictions and anomalies as the courts enter more and more deeply into the details of school administration.[9] There is, though, a larger issue of contradiction which quite transcends the problem of a mechanical accommodation to the requirement of dispersion of ethnic and racial groups, and the requirement, for purposes of enjoying a certain right, of concentration. Mechanical accommodation can be made that will perhaps satisfy lawyers for black and Hispanic plaintiffs. Can one, however, harmonize the larger objectives of both policies, which are also in contradiction? Dispersion aims at color blindness and group blindness. It breathes a hostility first toward concentrations created by state action which are intended to isolate a racial or ethnic group (and I share the same hostility), and second toward those concentrations that come about innocently of state intention as a result of residential concentrations of students of one or another ethnic or racial group. In this point of view we even find such concentrations that are the result of a desire by people to live in communities of common racial and ethnic background. To ignore that there are such desires, and that the resultant communities play an important role in the educational and economic advancement of ethnic and racial groups, and even make a contribution in time to their acculturation and assimilation, is to be ignorant of the history and sociology of ethnic and racial groups of this country. Alas, even judges are not immune to this ignorance, and thus are quite ready to break up communities of value to those who participate in them. As Judge Roth wrote in the Detroit desegregation decision, while trying to properly assess responsibility for concentrations of blacks:

> . . . if fault or blame is to be found it is that of the community as a whole, including of course the black community. We need not minimize the effect of the actions of federal, state, and local government officers and agencies . . . . to observe that blacks, like ethnic groups in the past, have tended to separate from the larger group and associate together. The ghetto is a place of confinement and a place of refuge. There is enough blame for everyone to share.[10]

In a word, desegregation law looks to a situation that I have, in other contexts, described as the evolving American ethnic pattern: In law and in public action, all Americans are to be treated as if they were stripped of their racial and ethnic attributes, as persons without any such group affiliations, history or influences. In a complex, multi-ethnic society, this is one possible adaptation. Race and ethnicity remain private, and the public sphere takes no account of them. Judge Roth is in this tradition, but he goes beyond it to intervene in and break up the communities that exist because of private action.

The Civil Rights Act of 1964 represented the high point of consensus on the emerging American ethnic pattern when it banned all discrimination on the basis of race and national origin. People were to be treated under a veil of ignorance as to their ethnic attributes. They were to be given neither more nor less because they were white Anglo-Saxons, blacks, Mexican Americans, Jews, or anything else. I think this hope, distorted by unwise policies that must subvert it, still can be detected in the language of the decisions that mandate treating children differently because of race and ethnicity. In both the desegregation decisions and the bilingual education decisions, the language is still that of "equal protection of the laws," and there is still the bland assertion that these measures, whether for the busing of school children on the basis of race, or for bilingual education on the basis of ethnicity and language background, are temporary. There is an expectation in the legal decisions, sometimes only vaguely discernible, that at some point all this ceases; that children will no longer be bused because they are white or black, and will no longer require a certain fixed curriculum because they speak Spanish at home. But in no decision that I know of, in no situation that I know of, is this vague expectation ever specified.

Indeed, the logic of the law is such that if a school system declared now to be unitary, or to be within the bounds of law in providing special education for the limited English-speaking, were, in its own judgment, to abandon busing or bilingual programs as no longer necessary, we can be sure it would be hauled before a court again for constitutional or statutory violations. Undoubtedly, the desegregation decisions point to the hope for an America in which race and ethnicity are private affairs, affecting the fate of neither individual nor group. The bilingual decisions suggest a different America, in which rights are affected by ethnicity and language, and in which, owing to the nature of the political process, it is hard to envisage a process which might result in declaring protections no longer necessary, thus allowing the state to withdraw. The lesser contradiction in the mechanical means of accommodating both desegregation and bilingual-bicultural educational programs in the same legal decree reflects the larger contradiction of what sort of ethnic America we have in mind.

There is a second contradiction between the line of educational decisions that we have been contemplating and educational objectives. It has turned out that what the Supreme Court and lesser courts demand are probably irrelevant to educational outcomes and may indeed in some measure be contradictory of them. One must be cautious—what the best qualified researchers and thinkers observe about what is educationally effective changes over time, and in any case can never be asserted as gospel. It is interesting to note, though, that the most influential recent work on what works in schools—work epitomized by Michael Rutter and his associates' *Fifteen Thousand Hours,* and which has reached the front pages of newspapers with James Coleman's first report on his research on high schools[11]—emphasizes as important for educational achievement themes that play no role in the desegregation and bilingual decisions, and indeed are contradicted by certain of their aspects.

First, we ask, does desegregation as such improve educational achievement? This much-studied issue still comes down to the conclusion—"no verdict." A recent compendium of research by proponents of strong desegregation measures comes up with no clear statement, though it tries hard to find positive outcomes (and in the variety of research that has been done in desegregation situations, there are undoubtedly many positive findings to be found). Willis D. Hawley, summarizing the position of those who argue for what I would call "hard" desegregation—that is, busing—asserts it is a myth that "desegregation generally does not enhance the academic achievement of minorities and may in some cases impede their learning." Despite his effort to explode this view,, however, (after all, it is labeled a myth), he concludes rather cautiously:

> In summary, Myth I is not generally true. While it is possible to identify circumstances in which the myth would be fulfilled, the evidence provides reason to believe that in most, if not all, communities it is possible to design and implement desegregation plans that will have positive effects on the achievement of minorities. But it is also clear that simply mixing children of different races will not necessarily bring positive results.[12]

One would conclude from this that the myth is not really a myth; instead, if one adds to a desegregation plan such additional educational features as new programs and new curricula, participation of local colleges and universities, teacher retraining and additional money from federal and state sources, one may find that educational achievement improves. It may also improve, of course, if one does all these things without busing. Under the circumstances, it is very unclear to what one should attribute the improvement in educational achievement of minorities when it is found. The situation with bilingual-bicultural education programs is similar. Early research showed no or minimal improvement in educational achievement.[13]

In the nature of the case there is no reason why one should expect otherwise. In the late 1960s and early 1970s, there was much emphasis in educational writing, experiment and observation on the importance of attitudes—the attitudes of teachers toward students, and of students toward themselves—as a determinant of educational achievement. Stigmatization of students by teachers would lead to a depreciated self-image which would affect learning. There is something in this, but far more was made of it than could legitimately be found. There have always been stigmatized minorities; some of them have done better in school (e.g., Jewish and Japanese students), and some worse. What truth there was in the stigma theory could not be easily affected by social policy. One finds that efforts to change behavior and attitudes through complex law suits are futile. Thus, the notorious Black English case in Ann Arbor resulted in the requirement that teachers be trained to be appreciative of Black English and to understand it as a different dialect; with their understanding, presumably, their attitudes toward their students would change, and the students would be able to learn better. That was the educational theory. There was no evidence that there was any true language barrier to communication: The children as well as their parents, as the judge pointed out, spoke standard English also. The only effect of the judicial intervention, which sent the teachers back to school to learn about English, must have been to lead the teachers to say with a shrug, "Well, if that's what the judge wants, he'll get it, and I won't bother too hard to correct what are errors in standard English and spelling."[14]

The desegregation and bilingual-bicultural decisions direct administrators' and teachers' attention to what is probably irrelevant to education, but they also have a more direct effect in inhibiting the kind of teaching and administrative style that the Rutter and Coleman research, and much else, suggests is best for learning. I will not summarize this research in detail, but two things among others seem crucial. One is the maintenance of discipline, and the other is the maintenance of an ethos that emphasizes learning: "The degree of academic emphasis, teacher actions in lessons, the availability of incentives and rewards [for academic achievement], good conditions in schools, and the extent to which children were able to take responsibility were all associated with significant outcome differences between schools."[15] The Rutter study emphasizes the significance of an ethos of learning in the school. It emphasizes such things as giving homework and carefully correcting it, agreement among teachers and administrators on the importance of academic work, and good and consistent discipline. The study also emphasizes the importance of teacher expectations and the use of praise.

It would be interesting to make a systematic contrast between the features that are emerging as significant for education and the features of judicial decisions affecting schools. This is a work for the future, but there are some very significant hints. On the whole, judicial intervention formalizes disciplinary code, emphasizes the rights of students, diminishes teacher and administrator authority, and reduces the degree to which students are to take responsibility for their actions. It replaces what has been an informal set of rules and expectations with a formalized one. The student entering the Boston schools is now given a handbook describing his rights; there is little or nothing in it about his responsibilities. Judicial intervention in this area flows from findings that black students or minority students may be disciplined more often than others, and from findings that some degree of due process has not been observed. The effect of such intervention is to reduce administrator and teacher authority, to increase the authority of lawyer representatives of parent groups and of specially appointed or elected parent committees—themselves subject to all the effects that make such groups more representative of those parents who are activist, angry, and resentful—and in effect to turn the school into a minor replica of the courtroom. Is this to the enhancement of learning? Hardly likely. One conclusion is clear: While an academic ethos and consistent and regular discipline are among the hallmarks of schools that enhance education, they play little role in the judicial and administrative decisions that have so deeply affected the schools.

The adversarial system of the courts regularly casts school authorities, administrators and teachers in the role of defendants, who, the lawyers charge, have committed a wrong. Undoubtedly many wrongs are committed, but the entire orientation of the legal approach is to emphasize actual and potential wrongs, and it finds it impossible to cast these wrongs into a balance in which the entire educational enterprise is judged. After all, that is not the role of the judge or the federal administrator. Their job is to uphold the Constitution, laws and regulations. As they do so, they inevitably give short shrift to the educational enterprise as a whole. It is true one of the objectives of this intervention is to improve educational achievement for minorities, but it cannot operate on the entire canvas of the schools (except in rare cases, such as in the Boston school desegregation); it is limited to correcting only those actions which are wrong in the light of the law. In doing so, intervention may indeed correct such actions, but it also unbalances the relations among administrators, teachers, students, parents and outside groups in the school—all to the detriment of education. The adversarial approach assumes that whatever the teacher and administrator do is done out of evil intent to harm minority children. No better example of this style of thinking is to be found than the decision of a California judge banning the use of I.Q. tests in the placement of black children in classes for those with educational deficiencies in California, and his requirement that minorities form no larger proportion of children in such classes than they form in the school population. Whether he believed these classes useful is not clear, but clearly he distrusted the judgment of teachers that they could help some children. Thus he required that a resource that had been developed for educational ends be statistically balanced regardless of individual need.[16]   One can now well imagine cases which argue that minorities must be proportionately represented in classes for the academically gifted (a case undoubtedly in which Japanese or Chinese intervenors would enter to protect the disproportionate placement of their own children in these classes.)

Judicial intervention does not mean that administrators administer better or teachers teach better. On the whole, I believe, it means both do worse. I say "I believe" because those studies that tell us what happens in the schools as the body of judge-set rules and requirements increases have not been done. In any case, whatever the impact of judicial requirements, we know what parents want. White and black, they want, overwhelmingly, better discipline, standard exams, more emphasis on basic education, more homework. At least the first three have been considerably hampered by judicial decisions claiming to act in the interests of minorities. Forty-five years ago, W.E.B. DuBois wrote:

> The Negro needs neither segregated schools nor mixed schools. What he needs is Education . . . . There is no magic, either in mixed schools or in segregated schools . . . . Other things being equal, the mixed school is the broader, more natural basis for the education of all youth . . . . But other things are not equal, and in that case, Sympathy, Knowledge and the Truth outweigh all . . . .[17]

Is this what judicial intervention encourages in the schools?

NOTES

[1] While the right to dispersion is entirely the product of judicial interpretation, and owes nothing to legislation—which has again and again tried, ineffectually, to limit judges in imposing this right—the right to bilingual education (and by this I mean the requirement that school authorities make it available—the question of whether eligible children must accept it has arisen but fortunately this degree of compulsion has not yet been imposed) has been created by an alliance of administrators interpreting legislation and judges interpreting the administrators' regulations and guidelines, and thus is not exclusively a judge-made right. This right is also viewed with consternation by legislators and Presidents. See Nathan Glazer, "Public Education and American Pluralism," in James S. Coleman, et. al., *Parents, Teachers and Children: Prospects for Choice in American Education* (San Francisco: Institute for Contemporary Studies, 1977), pp. 85-109.

[2] This description is based on visits to three schools (elementary, junior high and high school) in New York City, and on discussions with those administering or teaching in them.

[3] Bruce E. Cohen, in consultation with Peter D. Roos and Vilma S. Martinez, "The Co-existence of Bilingual-Bicultural Programs with School Desegregation Decrees" (Mexican-American Legal Defense and Educational Fund, no date), pp. 16-17.

[4] Ibid.

[5] One must smile at the naivete of judges reviewing school cases; the judges of the Tenth Circuit seem to think that bilingual instruction *prevents* "isolation of minority students."

[6] *Keyes v. School District No. 1, Denver* (II), 521 F.2d 489 (10th Cir. 1975), as given in Cohen, op. cit., p. 5.

[7] Peter D. Roos, "Bilingual Education: The Hispanic Response to Unequal Educational Opportunity," *Law and Contemporary Problems*, 42(Autumn 1978): 136-137.

[8] Cohen, op. cit., pp. 44-46.

[9] See Nathan Glazer, *Affirmative Discrimination* (New York: Basic Books, 1975, 1978), Chapter 3; N. Glazer, "Towards an Imperial Judiciary?" *The*

Public Interest, 41(Fall 1975): 104-123; N. Glazer, "Should Judges Administer Social Services?" *The Public Interest*, 50(Winter 1978): 64-80.

[10] Quoted in Glazer, *Affirmative Discrimination*, op. cit., p. 106.

[11] Michael Rutter and others, *Fifteen Thousand Hours: Secondary Schools and Their Effects on Children* (Cambridge, Mass.: Harvard University Press, 1979); and James Coleman, Thomas Hoffer and Sally Kilgore, *Public and Private Schools: A Report to the National Center for Education Statistics* (Chicago: National Opinion Research Center, 1981).

[12] Willis D. Hawley, "The New Mythology of School Desegregation," *Law and Contemporary Problems*, 42(August 1978): 217, 219.

[13] See Noel Epstein, *Language, Ethnicity, and the Schools: Policy Alternatives for Bilingual-Bicultural Education* (Washington, D.C.: Institute for Educational Leadership, 1977).

[14] See Nathan Glazer, "Black English and Reluctant Judges," *The Public Interest*, 62(Winter 1981): 40-54. There is a substantial literature on this case and its implications. See Geneva Smitherman, ed., *Black English and the Education of Black Children: Proceedings of the National Invitational Symposium on the King Decision* (Detroit: Center for Black Studies at Wayne State University, 1981).

[15] Rutter, op. cit., p. 178.

[16] Nathan Glazer, "I.Q. on Trial," *Commentary* (June 1981).

[17] W.E.B. DuBois, "Does the Negro Need Separate Schools?" *Journal of Negro Education*, 4(1935): 328, quoted in Cohen, op. cit.

ETHNIC GROUP INTERESTS AND THE SOCIAL GOOD: LAW AND LANGUAGE IN EDUCATION*

Richard Ruiz

University of Wisconsin-Madison

The question at issue is broad, so I have chosen to focus it in a way that draws attention to the complexities of cultural diversity in the United States. This question is: How are ethnic group interests in education promoted by law, and what relation might this promotion have to the "larger social good"? There is much discussion of the problems raised by school desegregation, affirmative action, and the role of the judiciary in resolving these; there is sometimes also a tendency to concentrate on issues of race and its importance in our representation of "ethnicity." This emphasis is important, and I do not mean to minimize it. (After all, Homer Plessy was only one-eighth black—a fact which attests to the tremendous salience of black-white distinctions in society and in law.) My objection is that we tend to forget other aspects of ethnic identification which, indeed, may be as significant as race in the context of schooling.

I am referring here to language. Our census enumerators tell us that the largest minority group in the country will soon be non-English speaking. By the end of this century, blacks will be overtaken numerically by Hispanics, by which is meant primarily Chicanos, Puerto Ricans and Cubans, though other Latin Americans and Europeans are also sometimes included in this category. Moreover, while the general school enrollment is decreasing, greater numbers of Hispanic children are attending public schools. This means that the demands on the school to address linguistic diversity will intensify. There is already a large body of codified state and federal policy, as well as court decisions, dealing with the responsibility of the school in this area. Before proceeding, however, let me elaborate our primary question.

What Are Interests?

A debate about ethnic group interests, whether they relate to race, language, national origin, or some other dimension of ethnicity, has little value without first sorting out what is meant by "interests." The articulation, aggregation and promotion of interests involve first a determination of what interests are; only then might we turn to the question of how law promotes them, and how this relates to the "larger social good."

Are "interests" to be construed as social goods by those who hold them? Is everything which I think will benefit me "in my interest"? Or are there other, more general standards by which we can evaluate whether something we consider desirable is actually an interest? How and by whom are my interests determined? Let us suppose that a group of us who are Hispanics would like our children to speak Spanish as we and our parents do, because it would strengthen the familial bond and allow succeeding generations to retain something of their heritage. No claims are made that our children will be better citizens, achieve at a greater level in school, get better jobs, or in any other way "improve themselves" as a result of that ability. How can I investigate if such language facility is "in our interest"? One might postulate that because we hold it as a social good, it is therefore in our interest. In this view, interests are social constructions to be evaluated by the group in which they emerge. Implicit in this argument is the assumption that the group itself determines what is in its interest, regardless of perceptions to the contrary from the outside.

On the other hand, we might decide that interests sometimes do not correspond neatly to socially determined desirabilities; that what is truly in one's interest will have to be measured by the eventual benefit it has for the whole group. Besides, it is seldom true that even small social groups can agree on what is desirable. When there are conflicting perceptions of what is desirable, interest must be evaluated by some external criterion. At any rate, none of this implies that one must create laws to promote one's interests, however they may be determined. That is because an "interest" is not compelling in the context of law. The concept must be translated (or at least translatable) into language forms which are. It may be possible, for example, to reformulate "interests" as "rights," a word which forces itself on the legal and legislative system.

Can an "interest" be construed as a "right"? If so, what kind of right is it? A human right?[1] A cultural right? An individual right?[2] A moral right? A legal right? And, as a right, what is its ontological status? Is it natural, and therefore inalienable? Or is it conferred on one by one's "group, and thus alienable?" Are not some aspects of human experience sometimes weakly represented as "interests" when they should be strongly affirmed as "rights"?

These questions are significant when asked in the face of what appear to be ethnic group demands. Some arguments for bilingual education, for example, are based on the premise that some interests are actually rights. Thus, bilingual education programs are demanded for reasons in addition to the belief that they will accommodate the legal (if not moral) right of children to equal educational opportunity, without discrimination based on national origin. Such programs are also linked to the right of self-expression and self-identification—construed as a natural and inalienable right—which is denied by not allowing the use of one's native language in school. This is a significant dimension to the argument identifying "interests" with "rights," for even where opportunities are equalized and discrimination has disappeared, the justification for bilingual education is not weakened. Advocated in this way, bilingual education—in its role of institutionalizing language maintenance—takes on the force of a natural right.

At the heart of the concept of rights is the question of claims. To have a right, according to Feinberg,[4] is to have at least a "claim-to" something. This claim-to can be justified in a variety of ways, depending on the substance of the claim. For example, if it is a claim about some legal entitlement, appeal to legal rules or principles (as opposed to, let us say, moral precepts) can make the claim valid. For Feinberg, however, this is not enough to make the claim constitute a "full-fledged right"; what is needed are both a valid claim-to and a valid claim-against.[5] To restrict oneself to a claim-to is to diminish what could be a full-fledged right into a "manifesto right." In terms we have already used, to affirm a manifesto right may be tantamount to expressing an interest, at least for the purpose of legal persuasion. Neither a mere claim-to nor an interest appears to have much legal weight. It is important to consider whether the demand for bilingual education constitutes merely a manifesto right, or whether it can be expressed more forcefully.[6]

Can an interest (and therefore a right) change with the passage of time and the advancement of knowledge? Apparently so, judging from the way the Supreme Court has overturned its own seemingly immutable principles concerning rights. Take the *Brown* decision nullifying the "separate but equal" doctrine. Did this mean that the interest of blacks was now different because of the judicial pronouncement? Or had the interest been there all along, denied or obscured by the Court's ignorance and misapplication of constitutional principles? On this point, Frederick Wirt and Michael Kirst say:

History threw little clear light on what the intent of the framers of the Fourteenth Amendment had been in this respect, but certainly the scope and importance of education had changed since then. Separation of children in this important aspect of their lives "generates a feeling of inferiority as to their status in the community that may affect their hearts and minds in a way unlikely ever to be undone." While such psychological knowledge may not have been available in 1896, it [is] today, so its weight should not be denied.[7]

So, an important justification for overturning long-standing judicial principles is that we now understand something about the human condition about which we were previously ignorant. In these cases, new knowledge about human development processes allows us to reassess what the ethnic group interest is: while before the Brown decision it was separate facilities, it is now propinquity.

The importance of *Lau v. Nichols* twenty years later lies in its reformulation of the principles underlying *Brown*. Its most startling pronouncement is that "there is no equality of treatment merely by providing the students with the same facilities, textbooks, teachers, and curriculum; for students who do not understand English are effectively foreclosed from any meaningful education."[8] This is no small thing; it calls into question the very framework which sustains *Brown*. Where *Brown* emphasized the importance of physical proximity in alleviating educational disadvantage and discrimination, *Lau* subordinates all this to the nature of the treatment, saying that disregarding such cultural variables as language can do as much harm as segregation.

In these changes, the Court has been reasonable. The fundamental tenet of *Brown* is that intentional separation of the races under state authority is unacceptable because it results in a radical disparity in resource allocation. *Lau* constitutes a refinement of that principle, rather than a negation of it. Sharing the same facilities is not enough to insure equal access to education; there must also be a reasonable attempt to provide services to children in light of their differences. To treat them all the same is, under *Lau*, to treat them unequally. Once again, we see here that judicial decisions based on new knowledge—in this case, about linguistic difference and access to curricular information—changed our conception of what constituted ethnic group interest.

If an interest is not a right, how does it relate to rights? Does it, should it, *inform* rights? These are not pointless questions for the world of schools today. In the case of bilingual education, the sociolinguistic literature on language attitudes and their importance in establishing a school program[9] may throw some light on the question of interests and rights. The critical point made by sociolinguists is that the general goals of the school program—either toward language maintenance or language shift and, indeed, the establishment of any program in the first place—should be determined primarily by the attitude of the parents of prospective participants. Consider two communities, one where the attitudes of parents are favorable toward a maintenance-bilingual program, and one where the parents want no special program at all. Does this mean that the right for a bilingual program has been created, or at least influenced, by the interest of the first group; while for the second—lacking the self-determined interest—no such right exists?[10]

This question is not farfetched. It is consistent with many of the arguments favoring bilingual education for some groups, but not for others, and it is a response to the contention that providing bilingual services in schools for one or two groups will open the floodgates of demand for such benefits from every conceivable language group even though it is possible that many, maybe most, of these groups do not see these services as "in their interest," preferring over anything else that their children learn English. Gaarder's characterization of the Norwegian attitude at the turn of the century indicates this lack of support for school-based language teaching: "Norwegian Americans—most of them—cherished their mother tongue, but Haugen found that they stoutly resisted those who advocated parochial or other schools that would have segregated their children from other Americans."[11] Whether or not one believes that rights should be informed by interests in this way, it is unsound public policy to insist on this benefit for those who would see it as a hindrance. The objection, then, that the costs for providing all these groups with bilingual education would be astronomical, because of the number of language groups potentially involved, distracts us from more pertinent questions about bilingual education. (Arguments that nativist rights should take precedence over immigrant rights are intimately related to this line of reasoning; it is to be expected, after all, that voluntary immigrants would make fewer demands for language and cultural maintenance than would conquered or colonized nativist groups.)

Underlying most of the formulations of "interest" and "right" discussed here is the notion that the particular interest and the general interest are natural competitors; the implication for policymakers is that the primary task is to choose between a particular interest and the greater social good. This is unfortunate. While in order to provide for the possibility of legal remedy "interest" language should perhaps be translated into "rights" language, a more beneficial approach would be to develop a language repertoire, the most important of which could be a "resource language." If instead of insisting on this or that right we were able to demonstrate the resource potential of cultural and linguistic diversity, the arguments about bilingual education would take on a completely different character. Questions of whether this or that linguistic group should be offered the privilege of language instruction in the schools would be subordinated to questions of resource development and management; more importantly, policy formulation would include strategies for using these resources in the best possible way, rather than arguments about whether we need them at all.

Just what is involved in developing such a resource language shall be discussed in the last section of this chapter. What we must remember is that if we continually regard interests as either particular or general, then we fail to ask the right questions about interests.

How Does the Law Promote or Hinder Interests?

Wirt and Kirst see the role of the judiciary in promoting or hindering interests as greater than merely that of arbiter in legal disputes. The Supreme Court, in particular, is important in that it gives not only laws but norms and values as well:

> The Supreme Court legitimizes national policies and values they reflect . . . In the process, the judiciary provides signals to litigants, general public, and political subsystems and their actors (including their own local courts) as to the policy-value output it will reinforce . . . . However such decisions are derived, they constitute outputs for society. They are something more than a statement of which litigant won and lost. Rather, they instruct a larger circle as to the value norms that the judicial subsystems seek to impose upon the environment.[12]

In the realm of language, judicial decisions as well as laws and legislative declarations contribute to the development of what Shirley Heath calls a language ideology.[13] The ideology is developed explicitly in the language of the pronouncement or implicitly in the orientation conveyed in making the pronouncement. Several examples of each will help to clarify this concept.

Both federal and state legislation on bilingual education is overwhelmingly transitional and compensatory, being aimed at children with identifiable "limitations."[14] The original version of Title VII in 1967 specified not only a non-English primary language but also poverty (that is, less than $3,000 income per year per family) as eligibility criteria for bilingual programs. Thus, the association between non-English language ability and poverty was embodied in a national declaration of policy.[15] This is not to say that the association was not already present in American language ideology, but the program language served to make the connection explicit.

Another example is the language of the Massachusetts Transitional Bilingual Education Act of 1972, the first such law and a model for many other states: "The General Court believes that a compensatory program of transitional bilingual education can meet the needs of [limited English-speaking] children and facilitate their integration into the regular public school curriculum." The law associates a lack of English language ability with a need for remediation, expressly stating that the program will no longer be necessary once a child has mastered enough English to become integrated with the "regular" school program.

Wisconsin's Bilingual-Bicultural Education Law (1975) is very similar to the Massachusetts law in this respect, even though it does not contain the word "transitional": "It is the policy of this state that a limited-English speaking pupil participate in a bilingual-bicultural education program only until such time as the pupil is able to perform ordinary classwork in English." Also noteworthy for our discussion of language ideology are two more things in the Wisconsin law. First, it is probably not insignificant that this statute appears in the Wisconsin Code as a subchapter to a larger section on handicapped children. The negative association with special education conveyed in the context of bilingual education is not at all subtle; it shows a definite attitude on the part of the legislators toward this kind of school program.

Second, in a list of definitions, most of the people involved in the programs are referred to as "bilingual": bilingual teacher, bilingual counselor, bilingual teacher's aide, bilingual counselor's aide. In the context of the statute, however, "bilingual" does not refer to language ability; it is merely a status marker conferred through certification. At the same time a student participant in the program is called "limited-English speaking . . . because of the use of a non-English language in his or her family or in his or her daily, nonschool surrounding . . ." This is ironic, suggesting the possibility of a classroom where the only person who has a natural bilingual experience is called "limited," while others—who are not necessarily bilingual but have passed courses and achieved a minimum test score, though not necessarily a minimum level of functional language use—are called "bilingual."

Here one observes an aspect of American language ideology which is as of yet merely an intuition: *adding* a foreign language to English is associated with erudition, social and economic status and, perhaps, even patriotism (consider that the military has been our most vigorous language trainer in the last thirty years—most of the trainees being native English speakers); but *maintaining* a non-English language implies disadvantage, poverty, low achievement and disloyalty (it promotes biculturalism and irredentism, both potentially politically dangerous). One's intuition is strengthened by the fact that evaluations of bilingual education programs show a tendency to be disproportionately impressed with relatively meager gains in Spanish language scores by English-speaking children when compared to the much greater gains on English test scores by non-English-speaking children. "Additive" bilingualism is acceptable when the second language is not English, but "subtractive" bilingualism is our goal when it is. Gaarder's contention that almost all Spanish-English bilinguals in the United States are mother-tongue speakers of Spanish[16] is probably adaptable to any non-English language speech community.

One comes away with the attitude that it would be a shame indeed if one's child were even *thought* to need a program of this sort. It is designed for people who have a problem—the ability to speak a non-English language. Moreover, the specific associations that one is invited to make direct one to conceptualize a dilemma on the horns of which only non-English language speakers are caught: one can retain one's language and culture, and thereby virtually insure economic and social marginality, or one can discard the old for the new and find oneself on the crest of the wave toward modernity, economic viability and social status. The Wisconsin statute reminds us that this is "a society whose language is English,"[17] and President Reagan insists that "it is absolutely wrong and against [the] American concept to preserve native language and culture in school programs."[18] This is in keeping with what Charles Ferguson says about the perceived incompatibility of indigenization and modernization from the point of view of the English-speaking nations. Certainly a non-Western indigenous language like Thai or Fula is in itself incapable of representing technological advances to its speakers; the vernacular must be subordinated to a Western language—perhaps even eliminated—in the interest of progress. Haugen makes the same point in saying about U.S. immigrants that "if individuals or groups rejected English . . . they handicapped themselves, because they limited their chances for socioeconomic mobility and valuation as good citizens."[20] This is an assumption not shared by industrialized non-Western nations of which Japan is a notable example.

Imbedded orientations as an important aspect of language ideology are not always easily recognized partly because, since they frequently reflect prevailing social sentiment, they are not seen as "marked." A good example of this is the tone of the Supreme Court in *Meyer v. Nebraska*. A German teacher in a parochial school was convicted of violating a state law prohibiting instruction in a non-English language. The Supreme Court found that a Nebraska Supreme Court decision upholding the conviction was in violation of the due process clause of the Fourteenth Amendment, and reversed; but the attitude of the Court was tolerant of the social judgment at the basis of the law: "The desire of the legislature to foster a homogeneous people with American ideals . . . is easy to appreciate."[21] The simple message is that one cannot really be an American and advocate linguistic diversity.

Heath finds this orientation in judicial decisions throughout the twenties, when every state passed language laws, and extending into the anti-subversive movement of the fifties. During World War I, knowledge of a foreign language was believed to be "clearly harmful." Between 1919 and 1925, more than one thousand people, mostly aliens, were sentenced to jail for "subversive speech"; Heath attributes this to the idea of "inchoate crime," where "words were said which made people fear something would happen, although no action ensued. The speech people used made them socially dangerous."[22]

Furthermore, Heath finds that judicial decisions in this period were "based on the view that language is a predictor, or at least an indicator, of behavior."[23] This view is illustrated in the following passage from the Nebraska Supreme Court's affirmation of Meyer's conviction:

> The legislature had seen the baneful effects of permitting foreigners who had taken residence in this country to rear and educate their children in the language of their native land. The result of that condition was found to be inimical to our own safety. To allow the children of foreigners who had emigrated here, to be taught from early childhood the language of the country of their parents, was to rear them with that language as their mother tongue. It was to educate them so that they must always think in that language, and as a consequence, naturally inculcate in them the idea and sentiments foreign to the best interest of this country.[24]

We might interpret this perceived threat in one of two ways. The first has to do with the impression that some groups of people were ill-suited to living peacefully in a democracy because either the political and social circumstances prevailing in their country of origin inclined them toward attitudes harmful to American society, or they possessed biogenetic qualities which were considered undesirable and dangerous. This is the thrust of E. B. Cubberley's well-known statement: "Illiterate, docile, lacking in self-reliance and initiative, and not possessing the Anglo-Teutonic conceptions of law, order and government, their coming has served to dilute tremendously our national stock, and to corrupt our civic life."[25] Allowing "foreigners" to teach these social traits and to reinforce their own language in the schools could be seen as against the best interests of a democratic society.

Yet another interpretation is possible. One might conclude that the encouragement of ethnic identification through the institution of school was itself a social evil because collective diversity of any sort—regardless of the perceived similarity of the ideologies at its base—would eventually work to weaken a democracy. Instead, the country needed to process its immigrant stock socially, through the schools and other institutions, in order to develop a common and fundamental sense of identity. In this view, the eradication of the distinctive—cultural, linguistic, biogenetic, political or otherwise—in order to create a basic commonality is essential for the maintenance of democratic institutions.[26]

Some may argue that this latter interpretation is exaggerated, that if it ever existed, it surely does not have much force now. On the contrary, it is a possible explanation for the inordinate amount of controversy that language issues—bilingual education in particular—have generated in this country. Surely, if we were concerned merely with the cost of the program, or even its educational merits, the arguments would not be as impassioned as they now are. *Meyer v. Nebraska,* after all, involved language instruction in a private school; funding did not emerge as an issue. The same was true of the Bennett and Edwards Law controversies in Wisconsin and Illinois. Yet it is hard to find a case in the first part of this century to compare with those in passion.

Nor does this orientation confine itself to another era. A recent manifestation of our concern for linguistic diversity outside the public funding issue is *Garcia v. Gloor.*[27] Hector Garcia was an employee of Gloor Lumber and Supply Company in Brownsville, Texas. The company had a rule prohibiting employees from speaking Spanish on the job unless they were communicating with Spanish-speaking customers. Gloor employed some workers who were Spanish monolinguals, and the rule did not apply to them. Also, the rule did not apply during breaks. In 1975, Garcia was dismissed from his job for violating the rule; he had been asked by another Mexican American employee about an item requested by a customer, and he responded in Spanish. Alton Gloor, a company officer, overheard the exchange. Representatives of Gloor argued that there were sound business reasons for the rule, and that the question of discrimination on the basis of national origin was irrelevant to the case. These business reasons included:[28]

- English speaking customers objected to hearing Spanish spoken because they could not understand the entire transaction.

- All of the trade literature and pamphlets were in English; not Spanish.

- Employees would improve their English skills by being compelled to speak English where they otherwise would not; this would not only improve their efficiency as employees, but would expand their opportunities as citizens.

• The rule would permit supervisors, "who did not speak Spanish," to oversee their employees' performance better.

Other factors, however, are also important. More than 75 percent of the population in the business area served by Gloor are Hispanic, "and many of Gloor's customers wish to be waited on by a salesman who speaks Spanish."[29]

The determination of the court entailed a relatively narrow legal argument: "An employer's rule forbidding a bilingual employee to speak anything but English in public areas while on the job is not discrimination based on national origin. [Garcia] was discharged because having the ability to comply with his employer's rule, he did not do so."[30]

The court left the issue there, but more questions have to be asked. What kind of business is it that would discourage the use and maintenance among its employees of a language which 75 percent of its potential customers speak? There are ways to encourage speakers of other languages to speak English on the job without so drastic a measure. Devising some system (or encouraging bilingual employees like Garcia to devise it) in which employees would have an opportunity to use both of these commercially important languages in the work place would surely be better business.

And what of the fact that none of the supervisors at Gloor spoke Spanish? Would it not have helped them improve the business by encouraging bilingual exchanges, so that those overseeing the operation could become at least superficially familiar with the predominant language of communication in the area? Besides, since one could assume that a relatively large percentage of the transactions would be in Spanish, how could the supervisors possibly oversee, let alone evaluate, the performance of the employee?

These and other peculiarities of *Garcia* lead one to think that other factors are at work here. Without a better idea of the particulars of the case and the specific situation being litigated, one can only speculate. The fact that the court confined itself to the narrow constitutional issue is not in itself unreasonable, but some comment on oddities in a case is not uncommon. Nor was this decision completely devoid of such comment. In a statement of justification for the finding that Garcia voluntarily and intentionally violated a perfectly acceptable rule, the court showed its lack of expertise on the issue of bilingualism: "the language a person who is multilingual elects to speak at a particular time is by definition a matter of choice."[31] Apart from the fact that this statement can be true by reason of circularity (whatever anyone *elects* to do is of course a matter of choice), the court fails to recognize the importance of sociolinguistic cues in the speech behavior of bilinguals. It is not necessarily true that a bilingual person has a choice of language codes regardless of the context (bilinguals whose linguistic knowledge is balanced in every domain of social experience are very rare), and it is true that one can distinguish between the cognitive choices available to an individual as a result of knowledge of more than one code and the sociolinguistic options available to the individual within the particular context. In the case of Garcia speaking with another Spanish-speaking employee, one can well imagine that the choice involved is a much more difficult one than the court suggests.

The point of this discussion is to suggest that orientations toward languages—their acceptability in certain domains or generally, their relative status, their extra-linguistic concomitants, their political and ideological uses—and toward the people who speak them are frequently implicit in the decisions reached involving them. These orientations can have consequences for the kinds of policy advanced relating to ethnic and linguistic minority groups. We tend to remember the xenophobic reaction of the Court in *Meyer v. Nebraska* more than the fact that Meyer's conviction was reversed. The way the court says what it wants, regardless of the decision it may feel compelled to reach, can affect the way those involved in these decisions are seen and treated in the public domain.[32]

How Is the "Greater Social Good" Identified?

How have judicial decisions helped us to identify what is the "greater social good"? It is fair to say that the Court's concept of this "good" has varied in time. In some cases, it is clear that the arguments reflected prevailing sentiments (as in *Plessy* and *Meyer*), while in others, most notably *Brown*, the Court's decision caught the general public by considerable surprise. Some of the decisions create distinctions and conceptualizations which are significant for the affected classes, although they may go virtually unnoticed by the general public. In *Gong Lum v. Rice* in 1927, for example, the Supreme Court accepted the finding of a Mississippi court that, for the purposes of the public education laws, all those who were not white belonged to the "colored race." Lum had contended, following the argument in *Plessy*, that since there were no schools for Mongolians, she should be allowed to go to the white school.[33] The court's denial of her petition rendered her legally a "Negro" for the purpose of education.

More recently, in *Pete Hernandez Petitioner v. State of Texas* in 1954, Mexican Americans were established legally as "Caucasians"; in *Ross v. Eckels* in 1970, Chicanos were not differentiated from whites in a Houston school desegregation case. This means that school officials could, following *Gong Lum*, classify non-Anglos as black; before *Brown* this classification served the interests of radical segregationists. After *Brown*, in a practice alleged on numerous occasions, blacks could still be excluded from Anglo schools by combining them with Chicanos to fulfill desegregation orders. One's inference, cynical and distasteful as it is, must be that the Court still cannot bring itself to eradicate a long-held conception that separation of the races constitutes a big part of the "greater social good," even after *Brown*. Modern formulations of this pervasive orientation are just more subtle than before *Brown*. Earlier, social mood allowed judges to be more direct, as were Justices McReynolds and Butler in their dissenting opinion in *Missouri ex. rel. Gaines v. Canada* in 1938. Here the Court considered the Missouri Law School's denial of admission to Gaines (a black man):

> For a long time, Missouri has acted upon the view that the best interests of her people demand separation of whites and negroes in schools. Under the opinion just announced, I presume she may abandon her law school and thereby disadvantage her white citizens without improving petitioner's opportunities for legal instruction; or she may break down the settled practice concerning separate schools and thereby, as indicated by experience, damnify both races.[36]

It is not only the Supreme Court and the federal legislative bodies that influence the development of these orientations in policy and ideology. Local authorities can and do play an important role in the development of policy regarding ethnic groups. Consider these few examples:

(1) "No Spanish" rules in Southwestern schools (especially in Texas), where children are punished in a variety of ways if found speaking Spanish to anyone anywhere on the school grounds, were in effect well into the 1960s, and endure in isolated cases even now.[37]

(2) Sterilization laws have been aimed at, among others, poor black women. Between 1907 and 1928, twenty-one states passed laws for involuntary eugenic sterilization; at that time, these were considered one aspect of progressivism, and some important historical figures were prominent in the movement. The "greater social good" deriving from these policies had a number of dimensions: it would allow the society to rid itself of the "defective germ plasm" which was threatening to destroy the social fabric of the country in the wake of the new immigration; it would display the effectiveness of the new scientific efficiency in

social human engineering; and it would be in the best interests of the "inferior races" as well. Henry Garrett explains this last concept in his pamphlet *Breeding Down*:

> You can no more mix the two races and maintain the standards of white civilization than you can add 80 (the average I.Q. of Negroes) and 100 (the average I.Q. of Whites), divide by two and get 100. What you would get would be a race of 90s, and it is that 10 percent differential that spells the difference between a spire and a mud hut; 10 percent—or less—is the margin of civilization's profit; it is the difference between a cultured society and savagery. Therefore it follows that if miscegenation would be bad for white people, it would be bad for Negroes as well. For, if leadership is destroyed, all is destroyed.[38]

Clarence Karier asserts that Garrett's arguments were not out of line, in nature or in tone, with the prevalent social and scientific attitudes of the time.[39] He considers the work of many prominent scientists and statesmen—Thorndike, Terman, Jordan, Van Hise, Ross and others—to have contributed most to this orientation. The motivation for advocates of the eugenics movement seems to have been a belief that genetic engineering was indicative of greater scientific and social efficiency. Garrett's comment implies that the "greater social good" is best served by at least a strict separation of the races, if not the complete eradication of non-whites.

(3) Finally, the rash of legislation attempted and passed during the period of anti-Oriental agitation in the Western states aimed at a similar view of the social good. The Chinese Exclusion Act of 1882, the Alien Land Laws and the Immigration Act of the 1920s,[40] and a variety of local ordinances—such as the one passed by the San Francisco School Board in 1906[41]—which were designed to keep Orientals out of schools, if not out of jobs[42] and out of the country, demonstrated the judicial and legislative determinations of the "greater social good."

How Do We Develop A Resource Language?

Garrett's argument contains an important central idea which has become prominent in public policy formulations of the last twenty years: The "greater social good" *includes* the promotion of ethnic and racial group interests. According to Garrett, it was in the interest of the black man that he be kept in subordination to the white society, which was his protector and benefactor, since he had nothing of value—and quite a lot of harm—to contribute to it. This is only the most obvious formulation of the "trickle-down theory" of public policy; in it, the distinctiveness of ethnic and linguistic groups *in itself* is never seen as a resource, the promotion of which is important in any conceptualization of the greater social good.

I agree that ethnic group interests are an important part of the general welfare, but I take issue with the motivation which has propelled public policy based on it. What is wrong with the "separate but equal"[43] doctrine; what is wrong with the naive notion of integration in *Brown*; what is wrong with most educational and social policy designed to improve the lot of ethnic groups by equalizing opportunity; is that these ideas have always tended to deprecate the resources which already existed within ethnic communities and individuals. At the basis of enforced separation is the assumption of inferiority rather than the right to voluntary association with familiars; behind "integration" frequently is the paternalistic attitude cited by Levin: "Many blacks reject integration as a solution not because it is identified with false promises but also because it has ideological overtones that are an affront to Black dignity. As Floyd McKissick has suggested, the view that quality education can only take place in an integrated school seems to be based upon the degrading proposition: Mix Negroes with Negroes and you get stupidity."[44]

Even recent concerns with educational opportunity and bilingual education have behind them the view that the targeted populations have little of value in themselves. We have mistakenly tried to remedy what we took to be deficiencies in culture or language or social orientation through promotive policies based on erroneous assumptions. What are needed most urgently are policies aimed at developing and managing the resources which exist in ethnic communities—not their eradication. This can only promote the "greater social good" since it aims at the integration of the strengths of each group. In the cases I have elected to discuss, language is to be viewed as just such a resource. As a resource, we should consider it in our planning and management, always seeking the benefit of the greater collectivity.

But what, actually, has been our position toward language diversity? We have already seen some of that. Perhaps one of the strongest statements about our language attitude is made by Gerald Johnson. "No polyglot empire of the world has dared to be as ruthless in imposing a single language upon its whole population as was the liberal republic dedicated to the proposition that all men are created equal."[45] Charles Ferguson, a bit less passionately, says about the same thing: "America is the world's leader in quality research in first and second language acquisition, but it is probably the world's poorest consumer of that research."[46]

One might well ask at this point, so what? What harm have we done to ourselves by discouraging and actively eradicating non-English languages and non-Anglo American cultures? Is this not overwhelmed by the good it has brought us—political unity, technological advance, military superiority, social cohesion, educational achievement, economic strength, all beyond compare? The fact is that we may not now see the pervasive and long-term damage that oppressive homogenization has had, even in the areas just mentioned. Fishman, in a rousing call for bilingual education, suggests that heavy-handedness in the cultural realm may be more dangerous than abuse of the ecological balance. His are not arguments based solely on the affirmation of "manifesto rights" or on the importance of natural symmetry: ". . . any argument that bases itself only on the ethics and esthetics of diversity is, in our more advanced day and age, only half an argument. If natural diversity is so central to a truly human existence, then there must be some demonstrable loss or damage when and if the balance of nature is disturbed."[47]

What are some of these demonstrable losses? There have been indications here and there in the last twenty years that our ability to cope with the demands of a diverse world has diminished. Paul Simon cites an example of this which is intriguing yet terrifying in its implications.[48] He asks us to recall the incident which, in many of our minds, set the tone for the Cold War and, more generally, made reasonable the anti-Soviet sentiments which remain even now: Nikita Krushchev's threat, "We will bury you." Simon points out, however, that this is a distorted representation of what was said. "We will survive you" is more accurate. This is similar to, though much less humorous than, the embarrassment suffered by President Carter some years ago when his interpreter showed his ignorance of acceptable Polish usage before a group of dignitaries. The language resources at hand in each case were inadequate to meet the demands of important international situations. Simon sees this as a worsening national problem which can have serious consequences. He points to some obvious indicators that something has gone wrong:

- In 1974, only 4 percent of our high school graduates had two years of foreign language training.

- Before our involvement in Vietnam, there was no American-born specialist on Indochinese languages available to the military.

- The Foreign Service has no foreign language requirement. Simon notes that even most of those who patrol for the Immigration Service along the Mexico-Texas border cannot speak Spanish. "Is this a rational way to run that kind of operation?" he asks.[49]

We must remember that this is true at a time when we are classifying natural bilinguals as "handicapped" and developing school programs designed to eliminate their "language problem." It could not be more obvious that the "greater social good" is best approached by preserving these important and fragile resources. We must now take up the challenge Ferguson outlined for us in 1978:

> . . . the time is ripe, and perhaps long overdue, for some Americans . . . to devote thought and effort to the formulation of a national language policy or set of policies which could move us toward conservation of our present resources and the strengthening of our resources where necessary, to meet the foreseeable language needs of our nation, for its internal strength and for its proper role in the family of nations.[50]

These resources cannot be neglected much longer without lasting negative effects. While we have introduced here the idea of a "resource-language" to talk about cultural and linguistic maintenance, we must see the differences between these and material resources like coal and oil. We can leave the oil in the ground and it will still be there to use in a hundred years; the more we use it, and the more we use it unwisely, the less we have of it later. Just the opposite is true of language and culture. The more we use these, the more we have of them; but the longer we neglect their use, the closer we are to extinguishing them. That has already happened for some languages, and we may be starting to see the consequences. The world will end one day, and the overriding cause is more likely to be a shortage of such human resources as language and culture, which could aid in promoting international understanding, than a shortage of such physical resources as coal and oil.

Whether the policies resulting from this orientation toward human resources embody bilingual education as we now know it, or some other institutional program, is not in itself the crucial issue. Ultimately, what is surely necessary are laws and legislative pronouncements which give status to precious resources like language. As yet, the most liberal policy does not approach this orientation.

NOTES

* This chapter has profited greatly from my discussions with Shirley Brice Heath (to whom I am also indebted for giving me a copy of her 1979 paper) and Andrew Cohen. It would have been a better work had I talked with them more. I would also like to acknowledge the invaluable technical assistance of Sharon Lorusso and Marie Ruiz.

¹ For an elaboration of this concept and how it relates to "cultural rights," see United Nations Educational, Scientific, and Cultural Organization (UNESCO), *Cultural Rights as Human Rights*, Vol. 3, *Studies and Documents on Cultural Policies* (Paris: UNESCO, 1970). Cf. also Vladimir Kudryavtsev, "The Truth About Human Rights," *Human Rights*, 5(Winter 1976): 199. The political rhetoric about human rights, especially in the last five years, makes a dispassionate analysis of this concept very difficult. Tibor R. Machan, in "Some Recent Work in Human Rights Theory" (*American Philosophical Quarterly*, 17[April 1980]: 103-115), makes a good attempt at this review and analysis.

² See Ronald Dworkin, *Taking Rights Seriously* (Cambridge, Mass.: Harvard University Press, 1977). Dworkin conceives of rights as based on individual dignity and respect rather than on collective concerns. He describes rights as "trumps over collective goals" (p. xv).

³ UNESCO, op. cit., p. 85. Yehudi Cohen contends that "people do not derive their rights from the very fact that they are human. There are no inalienable individual human rights; people have always derived their rights from their groups." (Ibid., p. 80.) Yet the distinction between individual and group rights may be misleading, as these two sorts of rights are intimately connected. The distinction underlies Cohen's later statement that "one of the first things the Nazis had to do was to declare all the people that they were slaughtering as 'non-humans.' First, they deprived them of their citizenship, and citizenship is the social definition of being human in a particular group." (Ibid., p. 85.)
It is also probable that affirmation of group over individual rights is culturally, ideologically and politically determined. See Kudryavtsev, for example, for a Soviet view of human rights. "There are no human rights in the abstract, in isolation from society. A right is an opportunity guaranteed by the state to enjoy the social benefits and values existing in a given society. For this reason the one and the same right (for instance, the right to education) has an entirely different content in different historical and social circumstances." (Kudryavtsev, op. cit., p. 199.)

⁴ Reviewed in Rex Martin and James W. Nickel, "Recent Work on the Concept of Rights," *American Philosophical Quarterly*, 17(July 1980): 165-180.

⁵ This point is disputed by McCloskey in Martin and Nickel, ibid. McCloskey sees positive entitlements as the basis of rights. "Rights are explained positively as entitlements to do, have, enjoy, or have done, and not negatively, as something against others, or as something one ought to have."

⁶ There is another kind of right, which may be called a "negative right," that may be relevant here. See A. Bruce Gaarder, "Language Maintenance or Language Shift?" in W. F. Mackey and T. Andersson, eds., *Bilingualism in Early Childhood* (Rowley, Mass.: Newbury House Publishers, 1977), p. 10. Gaarder asserts that cultural pluralism entails "the right not to assimilate." For this to be a right in Feinberg's sense, it would have to be translated into a statement of affirmation. The right not to assimilate becomes, for example, the

(positive) right to affirm and maintain a distinct cultural and linguistic identity. Even then, however, it would be difficult to develop a "claim-against" formulation for cultural pluralism in Gaarder's sense.

[7] Frederick M. Wirt and Michael W. Kirst, *Political and Social Foundations of Education* (Berkeley, Cal.: McCutcheon, 1975), p. 179.

[8] *Lau v. Nichols*, 414 U.S. 566 (1974).

[9] Joshua A. Fishman and John Lovas, "Bilingual Education in a Sociolinguistic Perspective," in Bernard Spolsky, ed., *The Language Education of Minority Children* (Rowley, Mass.: Newbury House Publishers, 1977). For an extensive examination of the issues surrounding the concept of language attitude more generally, see the collection of essays in Roger Shuy and Ralph W. Fasold, *Language Attitudes: Current Trends and Prospects* (Washington, D.C.: Georgetown University Press, 1973).

[10] McCloskey (in Martin and Nickel, op. cit., p. 169) would argue that the right (or "entitlement" in his terms) continues to exist quite apart from anyone's will, including that of the right-holder. From the perspective of public policy, however, one might hold that in that case there is no compunction to provide the entitlement, which under the circumstances might be seen as an imposition.

[11] Gaarder, op. cit., p. 413.

[12] Wirt and Kirst, op. cit., pp. 175-176.

[13] Shirley Brice Heath, "Social History," *Bilingual Education: Current Perspectives*, Vol. 1, *Social Science* (Arlington, Va.: Center for Applied Linguistics, 1977).

[14] This is as true today as it was in 1967. See, for example, Alan Pifer, "Bilingual Education and the Hispanic Challenge," The *Annual Report, Carnegie Corporation of New York* (New York: Carnegie Corporation, 1979), p. 11. He says that bilingual education is a "means of correcting English language deficiencies in primary school children, with the rationale that it could help them make the transition from the mother tongue to English and promote assimilation into mainstream education . . . It has not had as its central aim the fostering and maintaining of competence in two languages . . . . "

[15] Joshua Fishman in *Bilingual Education: An International Sociological Perspective* (Rowley, Mass.: Newbury House Publishers, 1976), p. x, strongly criticizes this aspect of the law. "I note the totally unnatural, shameful, and, indeed, slanderous relationship between bilingual education and poverty or other societal dislocation which is still required by much of the Bilingual Education legislation in the United States."

[16] Gaarder, op. cit., p. 418.

[17] See also the language in *Lau v. Nichols*, 483 F. 2nd 799 (9th Cir. 1973).

[18] *Washington Post* (March 4, 1981), p. 5. Numerous examples of this attitude have appeared in the popular media since the enactment of bilingual education legislation; these show, perhaps, that the President's statement is representative of a relatively large segment of the American population. See, for instance, Ernest Cuneo, "Bilingual Teaching Is A Grave Error," *Long Island Press* (June 19, 1975), p. 18. He writes, "If the parents of these children are too lazy or too ignorant to learn the American language, they ought not to be voting citizens . . . The emphasis, therefore, should be upon teaching their chil-

dren the American language to overcome the disadvantage of their parents. The object of American schooling is to teach them to think as Americans, not to continue the customs of a different culture."

[19] Charles A. Ferguson, "Language and Global Interdependence," in E. Michael Gerli, James E. Alatis, and Richard I. Brod, eds., *Language in American Life: Proceedings of the Georgetown University - Modern Language Association Conference*, October 6-8, 1977 (Washington, D.C.: Georgetown University Press, 1978).

[20] Cited in Shirley Brice Heath and Frederick Mandabach, "Language Status Decisions and the Law in the United States," a paper prepared for *Progress in Language Planning: International Perspectives* (Wayne, N.J.: William Paterson College of New Jersey, 1979), pp. 21-22.

[21] *Meyer v. Nebraska*, 262 U.S. 402 (1923).

[22] Heath and Mandabach, op. cit., p. 18.

[23] Ibid.

[24] Cited in Herbert Teitelbaum and Richard J. Hiller, "The Legal Perspective," *Bilingual Education: Current Perspectives*, Vol. 3, *Law* (Arlington, Va.: Center for Applied Linguistics, 1977), p. 3.

[25] Quoted in Milton Gordon, *Assimilation in American Life: The Role of Race, Religion and National Origins* (New York: Oxford University Press, 1964), p. 98.

[26] See Joshua Fishman, et. al., *Language Loyalty in the United States: The Maintenance and Perpetuation of Non-English Mother Tongues by American Ethnic and Religious Groups* (The Hague: Mouton and Co., 1966), pp. 29ff, for some explanations of the loss of ethnic and linguistic distinctiveness in American society.

[27] *Garcia v. Gloor*, 628 F. 2nd 264 (1980).

[28] These "business reasons" are remarkably similar to the justification given by school administrators in the Southwest for "no Spanish" rules in the schools: English is the standard language in the United States and all citizens must learn it. The pupil's best interests are served if he speaks English well; English enhances his opportunity for education and employment while Spanish is a handicap. Proper English enables Mexican Americans to compete with Anglos. Teachers and Anglo pupils do not speak Spanish; it is impolite to speak a language not understood by all. (United States Commission on Civil Rights, *The Excluded Student: Educational Practices Affecting Mexican Americans in the Southwest, Report III* [Washington, D.C.: U.S. Government Printing Office, May 1972], p. 14.)

[29] This is a factor of some importance in a similar case in Oregon, *Hernandez v. Erlenbusch*, 368 F. Supp. 752 (D. Oregon 1973). Here, the district court found grounds for a claim of racial discrimination against Mexican Americans in a tavern's policy prohibiting the use of any foreign language at the bar. In this case, the fact that Mexican Americans made up one-fourth of the tavern's potential customers was an important aspect.

[30] *Garcia v. Gloor*, op. cit.

[31] Ibid.

[32] There is another way to explain the Court's apparent ambivalence in the decisions it reaches, especially those relating to controversial social issues. Some on the Court have seemingly held that there is, or should be, a difference between "equality before the law" and a more general social equality; the argument is that the Court should rule in strictly legal terms, without any consideration of the social and practical consequences. Note this tension in, for example, the expression of the Court in *Plessy v. Ferguson* (1896): "The 'Object' and purpose of the Fourteenth Amendment, according to the court, was to secure the 'absolute equality of the two races before the law.' But, wrote Justice Henry Billings Brown, 'in the nature of things it could not have been intended to abolish distinctions based on color, or to enforce social, as distinguished from political equality, or a commingling of the two races upon terms unsatisfactory to either'!" (Albert P. Blaustein and Clarence Clyde Ferguson, *Desegregation and the Law: The Meaning and Effect of the School Segregation Cases* [New York: Vintage Books, 1962], p. 96.)

[33] *Gong Lum v. Rice*, 275 U.S. 78 (1927). Cf. *Cummings v. Board* of *Education*, 175 U.S. 528 (1899), the first Supreme Court school segregation case. Black plaintiffs, also using *Plessy*, asked for an injunction closing white schools in Richmond County, Georgia, until a separate black school could be provided. The suit was dismissed, the Court contending that the proposed remedy would do harm to everyone and good to no one.

[34] Cited in Gaarder, op. cit., pp. 411-412.

[35] *Ross v. Eckels*, 434 F. 2nd 1140 (5th Cir. 1970).

[36] *Missouri ex. rel. Gaines v. Canada*, 305 U.S. 337 (1938).

[37] See Manuel Ramirez III and Alfredo Castaneda, *Cultural Democracy, Bicognitive Development and Education* (New York: Academic Press, 1974), pp. 21-24; and United States Commission on Civil Rights, op. cit., pp. 14-20. The second source reports the findings of a survey of Southwestern schools which included information on measures taken against students caught speaking Spanish. The following comments are a sample of some of these measures: "If we speak Spanish we had to pay five cents to the teacher or we had to stay after school . . . ;" "In the sixth grade, they kept a record of which if we spoke Spanish they would take it down and charge us a penny for every Spanish word. If we spoke more than one thousand words our parents would have to come to school and talk with the principal . . . ;" "If you'd be caught speaking Spanish you would be sent to the principal's office or given extra assignments to do as homework or probably made to stand by the wall during recess and after school . . . " There was similar treatment for other language groups. See, for example, Gaarder's reference (op. cit., p. 414) to "teachers in public schools . . . threatening the pupils with punishment for speaking Norwegian on the playgrounds." Nor have these practices been limited to a concern with language. Alan Pifer (op. cit., p. 10) cites other contributions of the school to discrimination against Hispanics: tracking Spanish speakers into low achievement classes; "classifying them as mentally retarded and emotionally disturbed"; "denigrating their Hispanic heritage"; "giving them the message that they cannot, or are not expected to, succeed."

[38] Quoted in Clarence J. Karier, "Testing for Order and Control in the Corporate Liberal State," *Educational Theory*, 22:2(1972): 154-180.

[39] Ibid.

[40] The printed media were important in this agitation. V. S. McClatchy, publisher of the *Sacramento Bee*, spent considerable time and resources fighting

Japanese immigration in California. In a brief delivered to the State Department on behalf of the Japanese Exclusion League of California (See Valentine Stuart McClatchy, *Four Anti-Japanese Pamphlets, 1919-1925* [New York: Arno Press, 1978], he cites the League's "Declaration of Principles," the first of which is: "Absolute exclusion for the future of all Japanese immigration, not only male, but female, and not only laborers, skilled and unskilled, but 'farmers' and men of small trades and professions as recommended by Theodore Roosevelt." In support, he points to Roosevelt's autobiography: "Let the arrangement between Japan and the United States be entirely reciprocal. Let the Japanese and Americans visit one another's countries with entire freedom as tourists, scholars, professors, sojourners for study or pleasure, or for purposes of international business, but keep out laborers, men who want to take up farms, men who want to go into the small trades, or even in professions where the work is of a non-international character: that is, keep out of Japan those Americans who wish to settle and become part of the resident working population, and keep out of America those Japanese who wish to adopt a similar attitude. This is the only wise and proper policy." (McClatchy, op. cit., pp. 104-105.)

[41] Yamato Ichihashi, *Japanese in the United States* (New York: Arno Press, 1969), pp. 234-244. See also Harry H. Kitano, *Japanese Americans: Evolution of a Subculture*, 2nd ed. (Englewood Cliffs, N.J.: Prentice Hall Publishers, 1976).

[42] Herbert Hill, "Anti-Oriental Agitation and the Rise of the Working Class Racism," *Society*, 10(January/February 1973): 43-54. Hill shows how organized labor was instrumental in diminishing the opportunities of Asian Americans in the work force. He chronicles mass meetings of otherwise competing groups like the Knights of Labor, the Anarcho-Communists of the International Working People's Association, and trade unions, whose purpose was Chinese expulsion from the labor force. He also describes the workings of the League of Deliverance whose boycott of Chinese-made goods and lobbying helped in the passage of the Chinese Exclusion Act of 1882. While these were grass roots efforts, they were facilitated by the support of such well-known labor leaders as Samuel Gompers.

[43] Wirt and Kirst would prefer the word "desegregation" in this context. Their distinction between desegregation ("an administrative, physical act") and integration ("the emotional and spiritual belief of men") is taken from *United States v. Texas*, 342 F. Supp. 28 (E. D. Texas 1971). (Wirt and Kirst, op. cit., p. 200.)

[44] Henry M. Levin, ed., *Community Control of Schools* (Washington, D.C.: The Brookings Institution, 1970), p. 7.

[45] Gerald W. Johnson, *Our English Heritage* (Philadelphia: J. P. Lippincott, 1949), pp. 118-119.

[46] Ferguson, op. cit., p. 31.

[47] Fishman, *Bilingual Education: An International Sociological Perspective*, op. cit., p. 6. Pifer calls for the same kind of demonstration more specifically about bilingual education. "Its very vulnerability to criticism on political grounds makes it especially incumbent upon this experiment to justify itself educationally. Nothing less will do justice to the needs of children from linguistic minorities and to the meaning of equal educational opportunity." (Pifer, op. cit., p. 5.)

[48] Paul Simon, "Language and National Policy," *Language in American Life*, op. cit., p. 109.

[49] Ibid., pp. 110-112.

[50] Ferguson, op. cit., p. 30.

REFERENCES

Blaustein, Albert P., and Ferguson, Clarence Clyde. *Desegregation and the Law: The Meaning and Effect of the School Segregation Cases.* New York: Vintage Books, 1962.

Cummings v. Board of Education, 175 U.S. 528, 1899.

Cuneo, Ernest. "Bilingual Teaching is a Grave Error." *Long Island Press*, June 19, 1975, p. 18.

Ferguson, Charles A., "Language and Global Interdependence." In *Language in American Life* (Proceedings of the Georgetown University-Modern Language Association Conference, October 6-8, 1977), E. Michael Gerli, James E. Alatis and Richard I. Brod (eds.), Washington D.C.: Georgetown University Press, 1978.

Fishman, Joshua A. *Bilingual Education: An International Sociological Perspective.* Rowley, Massachusetts: Newbury House Publishers, 1976.

Fishman, Joshua A., et al. *Language Loyalty in the United States: The Maintenance and Perpetuation of Non-English Mother Tongues by American Ethnic and Religious Groups.* The Hague: Mouton & Co., 1966.

Fishman, Joshua A., and Lovas, John. "Bilingual Education in a Sociolinguistic Perspective." In *The Language Education of Minority Children*, Bernard Spolsky (ed.). Rowley, Massachusetts: Newbury House Publishers, 1977.

Gaarder, A. Bruce. "Language Maintenance or Language Shift." In *Bilingualism in Early Childhood*, W. F. Mackey and T. Andersson (eds.). Rowley, Massachusetts: Newbury House Publishers, 1977.

Garcia v. Gloor, 618 F. 2d 264, 1980.

Gong Lum v. Rice, 275 U.S. 78, 1927.

Gordon, Milton. *Assimilation in American Life: The Role of Race, Religion, and National Origins.* New York: Oxford, 1964.

Heath, Shirley Brice. "Social History." In *Bilingual Education: Current Perspectives* (Volume 1: Social Science). Arlington, VA.: Center for Applied Linguistics, 1977.

Heath, Shirley Brice, and Mandabach, Frederick. "Language Status Decisions and the Law in the United States" (paper prepared for Progress in Language Planning: International Perspectives, William Paterson College of New Jersey), 1979.

Hernandez v. Erlenbusch, 368 F. Supp. 752, D. Ore., 1973

Hill, Herbert. "Anti-Oriental Agitation and the Rise of Working Class Racism." *Society 10*(2): 43-54, January/February, 1973.

Ichihashi, Yamato. *Japanese in the United States*. New York: Arno Press, 1969 (orig. 1932)

Johnson, Gerald W. *Our English Heritage*. Philadelphia: J. P. Lippincott, 1949.

Karier, Clarence J. "Testing for Order and Control in the Corporate Liberal State." *Educational Theory 22* (2): 154-180, 1972.

Kitano, Harry H. *Japanese Americans: Evolution of A Subculture* (2nd. edition). Englewood Cliffs: Prentice-Hall, 1976.

Kudryavtsev, Vladimir. "The Truth About Human Rights." *Human Rights 5:* 193-199, 1976.

Lau v. Nichols, 483 F. 2d 791, 9th Circuit, 1973.

Lau v. Nichols, 414 U.S.: 563, 1974.

Levin, Henry M. (ed.). *Community Control of Schools*. Washington D.C.: The Brookings Institution, 1970.

Machan, Tibor R. "Some Recent Work in Human Rights Theory." *American Philosophical Quarterly 17* (2): 103-115, April, 1980.

McClatchy, Valentine Stuart. *Four Anti-Japanese Pamphlets* (1919-1925). New York: Arno Press, 1978.

Martin, Rex, and Nickel, James W. "Recent Work on the Concept of Rights." *American Philosophical Quarterly 17* (3): 165-180, July, 1980.

Meyer v. Nebraska, 262 U.S. 390, 1923.

Missouri ex rel Gaines v. Canada, 305 U.S. 337, 1938.

Pifer, Alan. "Bilingual Education and the Hispanic Challenge" (The Report of the President). Reprinted from *The Annual Report, Carnegie Corporation of New York*, 1979.

Ramirez III, Manuel and Castaneda, Alfredo. *Cultural Democracy, Bicognitive Development, and Education*. New York: Academic Press, 1974.

"Reagan Denounces Carter's Proposed Rules on Bilingual Education." *Washington Post*, c5, March 4, 1981.

Ross v. Eckels, 434 F. 2d 1140, 5th Cir., 1970.

Shuy, Roger and Fasold, Ralph W. *Language Attitudes: Current Trends and Prospects*. Washington D.C., Georgetown University Press, 1973.

Simon, Paul. "Language and National Policy." In *Language in American Life* (Proceedings of the Georgetown University Modern Language Association Conference, October 6-8, 1977), E. Michael Gerli, James E. Alatis, and Richard I. Brod (eds.). Washington D.C.: Georgetown University Press, 1978.

Teitelbaum, Herbert and Hiller, Richard J. "The Legal Perspective." In *Bilingual Education: Current Perspectives* (Volume 3: Law). Arlington, VA.: Center for Applied Linguistics, 1977.

United Nations Educational, Scientific, and Cultural Organization (UNESCO). *Cultural Rights as Human Rights* (Volume 3: Studies and Documents on Cultural Policies). Paris: UNESCO, 1970.

United States v. Texas, 342 F. Supp. 24, E.D. Texas, 1971.

United States Commission on Civil Rights. *The Excluded Student: Educational Practices Affecting Mexican Americans in the Southwest*, Report III. Washington D.C.: U.S. Government Printing Office, May, 1972.

Wirt, Frederick M. and Kirst, Michael W.. *Political and Social Foundations of Education*. Berkeley: McCutheon, 1975.

THE CARROT AND THE STICK: TWIN APPROACHES TO ACHIEVING MINORITY EMPLOYMENT EQUALITY*

Cyrena N. Pondrom

Former Executive Director, Governor's Employment and Training Office
State of Wisconsin

During the late 1960s and throughout the 1970s, this nation undertook on two fronts activities of unprecedented scope aimed at relieving economic and social inequalities between whites and non-whites. Although ultimately much else was involved, the fundamental thrust of both sets of activities was to establish greater economic equality through assuring more, better paid, and higher-status minority employment. Activities on both fronts relied primarily on law—usually legislative, sometimes constitutional, and always, in implementation, administrative.

One set of activities which came, paradoxically, to be clustered under the rubric "affirmative action," was dominantly negative in thrust. Beginning with Title VII of the Civil Rights Act of 1964, continuing with Executive Order 11246 and culminating, perhaps, in Supreme Court decisions like *Griggs v. Duke Power Company*,[1] employers were barred from carrying out employee selection, retention and compensation procedures judged to be discriminatory either in intent or effect. A variety of related regulations have been added in the 1970s, most importantly the Uniform Guidelines on Employee Selection Procedures.[2]

Enforcement entailed the threat of substantial economic penalties, including employment with back pay for successful plaintiffs (and, sometimes, all others similarly situated) and, in the case of Executive Order 11246, threat of debarment from federal contracting. The Executive Order sought an affirmative stance by requiring that positive remedial actions be undertaken to overcome the impact of past discrimination, but fell short of its goal because of the widespread perception by employers that they were being required to undertake actions contrary to their preferences or to their economic or professional interests. Resentment was compounded by the fact that employers who took pride in being law-abiding and even progressive citizens felt themselves accused of breaking the law. For all its affirmative rhetoric, equal rights enforcement remained a negative tool.

Close to this time, the first of a retinue of other instruments aimed at enhancing the capabilities of the poor to compete successfully in the work force was being implemented. In 1962 Congress enacted the Manpower Development and Training Act (MDTA). It was followed by the Economic Opportunity Act of 1964 which set up the Office of Economic Opportunity. Both were superseded by the Comprehensive Employment and Training Act (CETA) in 1973 and its reauthorization in 1978. All of these programs were designed "to break down some of the social, political, and institutional barriers to full participation by the poor in the labor market and society at large." MDTA and CETA were specifically aimed at providing "work and training programs to upgrade the job skills of unemployed and underemployed workers."[3]

These programs rested on a thoroughly "affirmative" premise: employers "invest" in the most economically productive workers they can find and workers invest their skills in the job. Some people, including a large fraction of blacks, Hispanics and American Indians, are shut out of the labor market because the skills they have to invest do not attract employers when viewed in competition with all other available workers. Under such a theory, what is needed is human capital formation. If Congress enacts laws that support the formation of human capital among the least advantaged, these unemployed workers will be able to move successfully into the labor market without coercion of either the employer or employee.

This theory of improving human capital in order to improve economic opportunity particularly underlies the MDTA. At that time many believed unemployment was resulting from technological changes that rendered workers' skills obsolete or eliminated their jobs altogether. For those persons and others who were not trained for new technological roles, retraining and skill development seemed a partial answer.

As experience with such programs grew, others formulated the theory that the need for human capital formation was insufficient. Dual labor market theory suggested that the labor market actually functioned in the interests of employers by forcing more vulnerable groups of people into the secondary labor market—into short term, high turnover, low-skilled jobs in which employer investment could be kept low, employees easily replaced and opportunity for advancement extremely limited.[4] Despite the fact that the two theories differed significantly, many manpower field workers found the perspectives complementary. The workers with the lowest human capital to invest were more likely to be pushed into the secondary labor market or out of employmennt altogether, particularly when their problems were compounded by membership in groups which experienced economic discrimination—minorities, women and youth. An increase in human capital would make these groups less vulnerable; moreover, support services run concurrently with training programs could specifically help vulnerable individuals overcome attitudes inculcated by participation in the secondary labor market.

The existence and interaction of these two theories did have some implications for employment and training programs. Instead of aiming at the middle-class worker made "excess" by automation, lawmakers and practitioners concluded that the programs should have their greatest effect if focused on the structurally unemployed. This evaluation was separately motivated by widely published "scandals" of the well-to-do—or at least the not-really-needy—enrolled in CETA programs. The result in the 1978 CETA reauthorization was a highly targeted program in which strict limitations were set on the previous year's income of participants, and heavy priority was assigned to the unemployed and general relief recipients.

Because minorities had been disproportionately represented among families below the poverty level, the effect of increased targeting was to increase minority enrollment in employment and training programs. MDTA institutional-based training programs between 1965 and 1972, for example, enrolled 43.5 percent minorities; MDTA on-the-job training programs over the same time period enrolled 30.8 percent non-whites.[5] These figures are significantly above minority proportions in the work force, but more intense targeting increased even this representation. CETA programs for fiscal year 1980, for example, enrolled approximately 50 percent minorities in the three major adult programs: Title VI (countercyclical) Public Service Employment; Title II ABC training programs; and Title IID, the Public Service Employment program for the structurally unemployed.[6] Thus manpower programs, although not established with the avowed goal of achieving employment equality for ethnic and racial groups, actually affect the hiring of ethnic minority persons at least half the time. Such a record must at least equal that of equal employment opportunity enforcement efforts, which are divided among women, handicapped and veterans, as well as minority groups.

With these two parallel activities focused on improving employment opportunities for minorities over the last two decades, what have been the results? From this deceptively simple question emerges a set of related questions, none with simple (or uncontested) responses. Have minorities made economic gains? To what extent can changes in minority economic conditions be attributed to either affirmative action, jobs programs, or both? Can a monolithic "ethnic group interest" for which there is a single social good even be detected, or are the interests of some ethnic minorities at odds with the interests of others? And finally, is the social good the same for ethnic group and majority interests?

The course of recent political events has made discussion of ethnicity and public policy particularly urgent. Leaders of the new coalition in Washington have challenged the validity of affirmative action as well as employment and training programs. At the very least, participants in the debate over these policies should attempt to be clear about whose real economic interests are supported or jeopardized by which programs. At best, the debate may offer the opportunity to select or retain a combination of programs which are most effective at reaching the desired ends with the fewest correlative ill effects. It will be useful to look briefly in sequence at some of the evidence germane to each of these questions.

Economic Gains

When measured in absolute terms, there have been dramatic improvements in the economic condition of minorities in the United States in the last several decades. As the table below shows, 68 percent of black families in 1947 were estimated to have lived below the poverty level ($3,968 for a non-farm family of four, in 1970 dollars). By 1973 that percentage had dropped to 28 percent. During the same time period black family median income rose from $2,807 to $7,269, and the percentage of black families having an annual income of over $10,000 rose from 4 percent to 35 percent.

TABLE 1

COMPARATIVE ECONOMIC CIRCUMSTANCES OF BLACKS AND
WHITES: 1947 AND 1973

Category	1947		1973	
	Blacks	Whites	Blacks	Whites
Under $3,000 Income	54%	20%	16%	5%
Over $10,000 Income	4%	15%	35%	64%
Median Income	$2,807	$5,478	$7,269	$12,595
Families in Poverty	68%	24%	28%	7%

Source: "Table 1.6, Annual Income Among Black Families, 1947-1973: in Hilda H. Golden and Curt Tausley, "Minority Groups in the World of Work," in H. Roy Kaplan, ed., *American Minorities and Economic Opportunity* (Itasca, Ill.: F. E. Peacock Publishers, 1977), p. 17.

Black position *relative* to whites also rose in these years, but much more slowly. As the same chart indicates, white median income rose from $5,478 to $12,595, and the proportion of white families living in poverty dropped from 24 percent in 1947 to 7 percent in 1973. The median income of blacks was thus 51 percent of whites in 1947, and had crept up to 58 percent of white income in 1973 after reaching 61 percent in 1970. Chicanos and urban American Indians have had roughly parallel experiences. In 1970 Mexican Americans had reached a slightly higher proportion of the median family income for whites than had blacks ($7,117 or 69.5 percent, compared to $6,279 or 61.3 percent.)[7] Urban American Indians, in 1969, were also slightly ahead of blacks in terms of median family income: $7,566, as compared to $6,832 for urban blacks and $10,474 for urban whites.[8] (Reservation Indians, in contrast, trailed far behind with a median family income of only $4,088. Neither employment and training nor affirmative action programs have made a significant difference in solving the dilemmas of the reservation.)

The gap between minority and white median income has not been closed evenly across the economic spectrum. There was a steady shift between 1960 and 1970 from blue-collar to white-collar jobs for blacks.[9] The salary differential between black and white median income declines at the top end of the spectrum where the greatest educational background is required. Some studies show, for example, a higher average salary for black faculty than for white, after controlling for nature and source of degree, publications and institutional affiliation.[10] This differential benefit in economic advance by subgroups of minorities has a significant bearing on the answers to the questions posed here. This is a subject to which we shall return.

Sources of Minority Economic Advance

There has been an association of federal affirmative action, equal opportunity efforts and minority economic gains by both supporters of these programs and those who charge that they constitute improper preference. It may come as a surprise, then, to realize that there is no clear consensus (among either scholars or those speaking for minority interests) that affirmative action is the basis for minority economic gain. Quite the contrary. Speaking to the Special Subcommittee on Education of the U.S. House of Representatives, Norman Hill, on behalf of Bayard Ruskin and the A. Philip Randolph Institute, said: "Affirmative action, we are convinced, can only succeed when combined with programs which have as their objective a much more fundamental economic transformation than affirmative action could bring about."[11] Thus, far from being a source of prosperity, Hill perceived affirmative action to be much more important as a source of backlash, and he attributed the great economic gains for blacks in the 1960s to "the policies of economic growth and high employment promoted by the Johnson Administration."[12]

Much the same point was made by the Congressional Budget Office (CBO) in a report to Congress in July 1976. Noting that the unemployment rate of minorities is persistently higher than that of whites, in good times and bad, but particularly in bad, CBO representatives explained:

> There are a number of reasons—including discrimination, educational attainment and achievement, job location, and the situation of the labor market—for the higher unemployment rates experienced by non-whites. In general non-whites have less education and lower skill levels and thus they are more frequently in less skilled and lower paying jobs than whites. Moreover, even when their education and skill levels are equivalent to those of whites, non-whites have often been relegated to lower quality jobs because of labor market discrimination. Their relegation to lower paying jobs results in higher unemployment among non-whites because in these jobs employers and employees have little motivation to develop long-term attachments between jobs and workers. Thus turnover is frequent. Because these jobs are disproportionately at the margin of the job structure, they are only offered in numbers sufficient to result in low non-white unemployment during periods of very high demand for labor.[13]

To remedy the problem, the CBO called for "a combination of long- and short-term macroeconomic and targeted policy instruments. Untargeted macroeconomic instruments will not reduce that part of the gap that is caused by discrimination and the other reasons cited above."[14]

This line of reasoning, ultimately endorsed by Congress in the 1978 CETA reauthorization, illustrates the merging of dual labor market theory with human capital theory as a foundation for employment and training programs. This rationale recognizes explicitly the essential function in reducing discrimination of color-blind economic programs which operate on an incentive rather than a disincentive basis.

Elsewhere, the CBO again acknowledges that discrimination increases non-white unemployment both by limiting education and training opportunities, thereby affecting future employability in the work force, and by directly depressing the demand for non-whites in the labor market. "Federal anti-discrimination and affirmative action policies *probably* lower these effects," they wrote, "but a quantitative

assessment of the effects of existing programs on unemployment is uncertain. Data on the effects of existing programs on unemployment is
[sic] limited."[15]

At about the same time, a detailed analysis of the data that were
available yielded a judgment that was less equivocal. In *The Economics
of Enforcement of Title VII of the Civil Rights Act of 1964*, Andrea H.
Beller concluded:

> The evidence suggests that in the aggregate, from its inception
> through fiscal year 1970, enforcement of Title VII at best left the
> economic position of black males unchanged and at worst caused
> it to deteriorate. While enforcement of the employment provision
> increased relative employment in covered firms and relative em-
> ployment and wages in the economy, enforcement of the wage
> provision had precisely the opposite effects. The latter effects ap-
> pear to have dominated the former, although the net negative im-
> pact is, in general, statistically insignificant.[16]

Two years later, Richard Butler and James Heckman subjected existing studies of the impact of equal opportunity programs to intensive
scrutiny. They found that "there [was] no evidence that government
anti-discrimination policy [had] had any impact on eliminating black-
white wage differentials."[17] Instead, they believe, analyses supporting
the effectiveness of government anti-discrimination policies have focused on labor demand and have ignored concurrent policies affecting
labor supply. Specifically, the authors feel increases in black wages are
more likely to derive from a reduction in the number of black laborers
willing to work at low wage rates than from an increased demand for
black labor. The former would result from income transfer policies, and
the latter from anti-discrimination policies. A reduction in black participation in the work force during this time period supports their
view.[18]

The authors focus on income transfer payments. Similar effects
could be generated by other aspects of employment and training programs such as the increase in human capital resulting from increased
training, although Butler and Heckman do not address these. Such an
increase can be documented by an examination of the "Continuous
Longitudinal Manpower Survey" and the "CETA Quarterly Survey of
Participant Characteristics." The latter report also documents the
fact that minorities benefit from those programs in numbers disproportionate to their representation in the general population or the labor
force. (Such disproportionate participation is the requirement identified by the CBO for government policies to serve to combat the effects
of discrimination.)[19] Evidence for these assertions is laid out in Tables
2 and 3.

Table 2 identifies the number and percentage of minorities and whites terminating from five principal adult CETA programs in fiscal year 1980, and the number and percentage entering employment. From 40 percent to 55 percent of the participants entering employment in each of the five programs were minorities. In the same year, 12,548,000 of the total civilian work force of 104,719,000, or 12 percent, were minorities.[20]

Table 3 shows the increase in the pre- and post-CETA median wage of CETA participants entering employment in 1980. In Title VI the wages increased from $3.36 to $4.26 an hour. For Title II ABC, wages rose from $3.11 to $3.76; in the Governor's Grants Program the increase was from $3.32 to $3.60; and in Title IID median wages rose from $3.17 to $4.02.

(See Table 2, page 82.)

TABLE 2
SUMMARY OF FISCAL YEAR 1980 DATA ON CETA
PARTICIPANTS****

Title	II ABC	II D	VI	VII	Governor's Grants
Total Terminations	780,569	282,943	280,761	32,914	55,887
Total Entered Employment	289,186	87,988	84,929	13,915	20,458
Percentage of All Terminees Entering Employment	37.05%	31.10%	30.25%	42.28%	36.61%
Terminations - White	378,679 [48.5]**	144,148 [50.9]	145,995 [52.0]	15,400 [46.8]	21,774 [39.0]
Entered Employment - White	151,813 [52.5]***	52,508 [59.7]	51,016 [60.1]	6,845 [49.2]	9,226 [45.1]
Percentage of Terminees Entering Employment - White	40.09%	36.43%	34.9%	44.45%	42.37%
Terminations - Black	263,007 [33.7]**	91,771 [32.4]	91,272 [32.5]	10,797 [32.8]	23,398 [41.9]
Entered Employment - Black	81,539 [28.2]***	23,069 [26.2]	21,492 [25.3]	4,068 [29.2]	6,274 [30.7]
Percentage of Terminees Entering Employment - Black	31.0%	25.14%	23.6%	37.68%	26.81%
Terminations - Hispanic	105,290 [13.5]**	34,552 [12.2]	31,183 [11.1]	5,036 [15.3]	8,857 [15.8]
Entered Employment - Hispanic	42,258 [14.6]***	9,633 [10.9]	9,729 [11.5]	2,159 [15.5]	4,328 [21.2]
Percentage of Terminees Entering Employment - Hispanic	40.13%	27.88%	31.2%	42.87%	48.87%
Terminations - American Indian or Alaskan Native	11,940 [1.5]**	7,599 [2.7]	7,898 [2.8]	511 [1.6]	628 [1.1]
Entered Employment - American Indian or Alaskan Native	3,492 [1.2]***	1,407 [1.6]	1,212 [1.4]	203 [1.5]	198 [1.0]
Percentage of Terminees Entering Employment - American Indian or Alaskan Native	29.25%	14.66%	15.3%	39.73%	31.53%
Terminations - Asian or Pacific Islander	21,653 [2.8]**	4,873 [1.7]	4,413 [1.6]	1,170 [3.6]	1,230 [2.2]
Entered Employment - Asian or Pacific Islander	10,084 [3.5]***	1,371 [1.6]	1,480 [1.7]	640 [4.6]	432 [2.1]
Percentage of Terminees Entering Employment - Asian or Pacific Islander	46.57%	28.13%	33.5%	54.70%	35.12%

** The bracketed percentage represents the share of all terminations by title that fall into the specific ethnic category.

*** The bracketed percentage represents the share of all those entering employment by title that fall into the specific ethnic category.

****Source: "Quarterly Summary of Participant Characteristics: Fourth Quarter (FINAL), Fiscal Year 1980." Issued by the U.S. Department of Labor, April 10, 1981. I wish to thank Mr. Harvey Sokolow for securing this unpublished report and summarizing its contents in the foregoing chart.

TABLE 3
PRE- AND POST-CETA WAGES OF CETA TERMINEES

Wages of Terminees Entering Employment	Before Participation		Upon Employment	
	Number	Percentage of Wage Earners	Number	Percentage of Wage Earners
TITLE VI PROGRAM				
No previous wage	13,926			
Less than $3.11	26,459	42.6	10,958	14.6
$3.11 - $3.49	6,,870	11.1	8,595	11.4
$3.50 - $3.99	8,583	13.8	12,399	16.5
$4.00 - $4.99	9,988	16.1	21,062	28.1
$5.00 - $5.99	4,967	8.0	11,543	15.4
$6.00 - or more	5,171	8.3	10,518	14.0
Median Wage	$3.36		$4.26	
TITLE II ABC PROGRAM				
No previous wage	68,250			
Less than $3.11	103,102	49.9	63,912	23.2
$3.11 - $3.49	26,100	12.6	44,664	16.2
$3.50 - $3.99	27,512	13.3	55,626	20.2
$4.00 - $4.99	25,987	12.6	63,860	23.2
$5.00 - $5.99	11,912	5.8	25,270	9.2
$6.00 - or more	12,175	5.9	21,921	8.0
Median Wage	$3.11		$3.76	
GOVERNOR'S GRANTS PROGRAM				
No previous wage	6,918			
Less than $3.11	5,493	42.4	6,173	30.6
$3.11 - $3.49	1,755	13.5	2,989	14.8
$3.50 - $3.99	2,465	19.0	4,193	20.8
$4.00 - $4.99	1,707	13.2	3,566	17.7
$5.00 - $5.99	785	6.1	1,651	8.2
$6.00 - or more	756	5.8	1,581	7.8
Median Wage	$3.32		$3.60	
TITLE IID PROGRAM				
No previous wage	15,942			
Less than $3.11	30,393	48.0	12,980	16.6
$3.11 - $3.49	7,085	11.2	11,090	14.2
$3.50 - $3.99	8,659	13.7	14,540	18.6
$4.00 - $4.99	8,734	13.8	21,469	27.5
$5.00 - $5.99	4,277	6.8	9,963	12.7
$6.00 - or more	4,161	6.6	8,148	10.4
Median Wage	$3.17		$4.02	

Source: U.S. Department of Labor, Employment and Training Administration, Summary of Participant Characteristics for quarter ending 9/30/80.

Long-term, post-program data confirm that these gains should continue. A report of research on May 20, 1981, indicates, "The average percent of time employed increased from 45 percent in the year before CETA enrollment to 60 per cent in the first post-CETA year and 67 percent in the second year after termination. Average annual earnings improved from $2,760 in the pre-CETA year to $4,250 in the first year after termination and $5,350 in the second post-CETA year—a relative gain of 94 percent over the pre-CETA year."[21] What is more, "groups with limited pre-program earnings—such as women, minorities, young people and others with poor employment histories—achieved the greatest percentage gains in annual earnings."[22]

Are Ethnic Group Interests Monolithic?

The foregoing data appear to show that low-income minority groups have an overriding interest in highly-targeted, color-blind programs designed to increase human capital and provide positive economic incentives for employers to incorporate minorities within the primary labor market. Of the programs currently available, the institutional and on-the-job training programs—Titles II ABC and VII—have the best record in placing minority candidates in employment after enrollment, albeit not the best post-program wage rates. Data on the economic impact of equal opportunity programs, while inconclusive, suggest that low-income minorities may justifiably have only a passive interest in equal opportunity programs, at least as an economic tool. The data support some practicioners' perceptions that equal opportunity programs are primarily middle-class, both in origin and in benefits.

There is evidence which suggests that there have been clear minority beneficiaries of affirmative action programs. Younger, more highly educated minority workers experience the smallest wage differential with whites. These individuals have been moving steadily into white-collar, upper-level jobs in greater numbers than ever before. These changes are clearly desirable, but it is controvertible whether they are occasioned by demand-side labor policies that rely upon equal opportunity regulations. Even more encouraging is the observation that the number of blacks going to college is higher than ever before, and is now proportionate to the number of whites attending college. The prospect, then, is bright for the continued movement of minorities into higher-paying professional positions.

These outcomes may very well be linked to equal opportunity efforts. In assessing what programs work, however, one should note that the increase in minority education has functioned much more like an incentive program to increase human capital than a disincentive program to bar discrimination. For example, at the college level, enforcement activities to require an increase in minority enrollments—apart from the celebrated dual school system cases—either have been limited or have attracted little attention.

A great increase in student financial aid for low-income students has, however, been very visible. This aid has offered incentives to students and colleges to increase minority college attendance. At the same time, college completion by minority students is, from the perspective of the labor market, an increase in human capital that acts as an incentive for employers to hire minority graduates. The post-college increase in earnings for these students is evidence that at this level, as in employment and training programs that function at the entry level, the incentive process is working.

To the extent that one attributes minority gains in education and employment to enforcement activities, poor and middle-income minorities may have different priorities for government programs. If, however, one concludes that incentives rather than enforcement are the driving force behind minority gains in higher education and professional jobs, one cannot but think anew about the sorts of programs that will be needed to maintain and expand those gains. It would appear that the carrot works better than the stick.

Ethnic Interests and the Social Good

Suppose all were to agree upon a common set of incentives that should be implemented. Could we pay for it? The data do not clearly support or rebut a primary contention of Reagan's economic policy. Presidential representatives maintain that virtually all social welfare programs—particularly those including employment and training programs—must be cut back in order to reduce taxes and government spending. Such steps are necessary, they claim, in order to curb inflation and fuel economic recovery; without them, they say, the poor will be worse off, even if they retain certain social benefits.

All available data support the contention that the poor and marginally employed suffer worst in recessions and inflation. In the May 1975 recession, minorities were the first laid off and the slowest to experience recovery. In October 1973, white unemployment was 4.2 percent. In May 1975 it was 8.3 percent; in June 1976 it was 6.8 percent. At the same three points non-white unemployment was 8.5 percent, 14.2 percent and 13.3 percent respectively.[23] The same pattern has been present in the current recession; in May 1980, Hispanic unemployment rates were 10.5 percent, black 14.7 percent and white 6.9 percent.[24]

Even in the best of times, however, minority employment trails white. Why should we expect that non-targeted macroeconomic policies today will be sufficient to make economic benefits equally available to all? Given the controvertibility of such policies, what calculations show that minority poor will be better off without such targeted programs because of improvement in the economy as a whole? It may well be that such policies will widen the gap between those with human capital—black, brown or white—and those without. The question must then move to a broader issue of what constitutes the social good—for individual groups and for all. Could it be, then, that the discussion should involve as much those who study poetry as the ones who study poverty and/or the law.

NOTES

* The author wishes to express particular thanks to three members of her staff who helped in the preparation of this paper: Harvey Solokow, who secured extensive materials for use in developing this analysis, and Nancy Gleason and Ellen Hansen, who organized the office so it was possible to get the paper typed.

[1] 401 U.S. 424(1971). In *Griggs*, the Supreme Court barred the use of general intelligence tests and other employment tests which had a disproportionate impact on minorities unless clear "business necessity" could be shown.

[2] CFR 1607 (1979). For a survey of these developments, see *Affirmative Action in the 1980's: Dismantling the Process of Discrimination*, A Proposed Statement of the United States Commission on Civil Rights (Washington, D.C.: Clearinghouse Publication 65, January 1981).

[3] Charles R. Perry, Bernard E. Anderson, Richard L. Rowan, Herbert R. Northrup, et. al., *The Impact of Government Manpower Programs In General, and on Minorities and Women*, Manpower and Human Resources Study, No. 4 (Philadelphia: University of Pennsylvania, 1975), p. 3. The volume is an excellent evaluation of the impact of MDTA and the 1973 CETA. For a review of the impact of the same programs, plus some views of the 1978 CETA, see Eli Ginzberg, ed., *Employing the Unemployed* (New York: Basic Books, 1980).

[4] See Peter B. Doeringer and Michael J. Piore, *Internal Labor Markets and Manpower Analyses* (Lexington, Mass.: D.C. Heath and Co., 1971).

[5] Perry et. al., op. cit., Table I-2, p. 22.

[6] *Quarterly Summary of Participant Characteristics, Fiscal Year 1980* (Washington, D.C.: U.S. Department of Labor, April 10, 1981), pp. 6673, 7747, 9269. Hereinafter this work is cited as *QSPC, 1980*.

[7] Excerpted from Hilda H. Golden and Curt Tausky, Table 1.10, in "Minority Groups in the World of Work," in H. Roy Kaplan, ed., *American Minorities and Economic Opportunity* (Itasca, Ill.: F. E. Peacock Publishers, 1977), p. 23.

[8] Sar A. Levitan, William B. Johnston, and Robert Taggart, *Minorities in the United States: Problems, Progress, and Prospects* (Washington, D.C.: Public Affairs Press, 1975), p. 83. The data base differs from that in the previous citation but the comparison remains useful nonetheless.

[9] Bart Landry, "The Economic Position of Black Americans," in Kaplan, op. cit., p. 76.

[10] Thomas Sowell, *Affirmative Action Reconsidered: Was It Necessary in Academia?* American Enterprise Institute Evaluative Studies 27 (Washington, D.C.: American Enterprise Institute for Public Policy Research, December 1975), pp. 15-23.

[11] Delivered September 17, 1974, and published separately by the A. Philip Randolph Institute.

[12] Ibid.

[13] David S. Mundel, et. al., *The Unemployment of Nonwhite Americans: The Effects of Alternative Policies,* Congressional Budget Office Background Paper No. 11 (Washington, D.C.: U.S. Government Printing Office, 1976).

[14] Ibid.

[15] Ibid., p. xv. Emphasis added.

[16] Andrea H. Beller, *The Economics of Enforcement of Title VII of the Civil Rights Act of 1964,* Institute for Research on Poverty Discussion Paper 313-75 (Madison, Wis.: Institute for Research on Poverty, October 1975), abstract page. The study was conducted on behalf of the U.S. Department of Labor.

[17] Richard Butler and James Heckman in Leonard J. Hauseman, et. al., eds., *Equal Rights and Industrial Relations* (Madison, Wis.: Industrial Relations Research Association, 1977), p. 267.

[18] Ibid. p. 236.

[19] *QSPC, 1980,* op. cit., p. xiv.

[20] *Employment and Earnings: U. S. Department of Labor Household Data, Annual Averages* (Washington, D.C.: Department of Labor, January 1981).

[21] *Employment and Training Reporter* (May 20, 1981): 1045.

[22] Ibid.

[23] Mundel, op. cit., p. xi.

[24] *Employment in Perspective: Minority Workers,* Report 616 (Washington, D.C.: U.S. Department of Labor, Bureau of Labor Statistics, Second Quarter, 1980), p. 1.

RACISM, SEXISM AND WORK: LEGAL AND POLITICAL STRATEGIES TOWARD THE EMPOWERMENT OF OPPRESSED LABORERS/TWO STUDIES

Manning Marable

Fisk University

The roots of racism are found within the particular evolution of the capitalist political economy in America. Black workers, from slavery prior to the Civil War, to the sharecropping and crop lien systems of agricultural production from 1865 up to the eve of the Second World War, into the period of modern industrial and commercial employment, have been the most oppressed sector of the working class. Similarly, women have been systematically denied equal opportunity of employment in virtually every level of the economic system. Black women in particular have been the victims of a double burden—race and sex. The major challenge that confronts American democracy, especially its legal and political systems, is the resolution of the systematic exploitation of, and discrimination against, blacks, ethnic minorities and women within the contextual framework of a more just and productive society.

This chapter will consider two distinct problems in contemporary political economy relating to the crisis of employment. The first is the systematic and deliberate discrimination against black women in the work force. The second is the loss of jobs within the Frostbelt, which is a manifestation of the flight of capital from one area of the nation to another. Both problems are structural in nature; that is, both are deeply rooted within the evolutionary development of the private market economy in the United States. The latter issue is far from being color-blind, because plant closings tend to affect older industrial sectors where black and Hispanic workers are highly represented in the work force. Solutions to both problems are available through the development of "non-reform reformist" programs and legal strategies aimed at empowering the traditionally powerless members of American society.

Racism and Sexism

Among the leading fighters in the struggle for Afro-American liberation
have always been black women. The tradition of militant, activist
black women runs deeply throughout the entire black experience—
from Harriet Tubman and Sojourner Truth in the nineteenth century,
to Ida Wells Barnett, Fannie Lou Hamer, Angela Davis, Barbara Size-
more and Willie Mae Reid in the twentieth. This is no historical acci-
dent. It is also no secret, however, that for many years sexism has been
a problem within the Freedom Movement. Black women who live
alone, or who are the sole parent figure within their families, are often
the victims of poverty and unemployment. Statistics from the March
1980 report of the Bureau of the Census reveal a pervasive pattern of
exploitation.

There are 2,430,000 black families or households where a husband is
not present. Of these families, 1,195,000 are below the poverty level
established by the federal government, a percentage (49.2) that is
slightly higher than that of Hispanics (49 percent), and much higher
than that of whites (30.1 percent). Black families are larger than white
or Hispanic families. The mean size of the black family with a female
head was 3.64 persons; for those black families below the poverty line,
the mean figure was 3.93 persons. This contrasts with white family
means of 2.86 persons and 3.22 persons, respectively. Black families
headed by women without a male present also tend to be somewhat
larger than those of white or Hispanic women. Here the statistics reveal what our experience with the cruel and harsh realities of poverty
tells us—that the more children black families led by women have, the
greater likelihood that the family will be poor. For example, the census
reported that there were 633,000 black families headed solely by
women that had three persons. Of this number, 293,000, or 46.2 percent, were below the poverty line. There were 244,000 black families
with women heads that had five persons in the household. Of this
group, 152,000, or 62.5 percent, were impoverished. For black families
with women household heads having seven or more persons in the
home, a staggering 68.6 percent (134,000 families) were below the poverty line.

Poverty is often a product of poor schools or lack of education.
333,000 black female family heads have less than an eighth grade education. Of this group, 173,000 or 52.1 percent live below the poverty
line. Of the 144,000 women with an educational level of grade eight,
ninety-six thousand or 66.9 percent live below the poverty level. Yet
because of the dual burden of race and class, black women who do excel
in education are far more frequently without work than their white or

Hispanic counterparts. 358,000 black female householders have attended one year or more of college. Of this number, ninety-six thousand or 26.7 percent, are below the poverty line. This percentage exceeds that for Hispanics (19 percent) and for whites (10.7 percent).

Millions of black and brown women were pressured into the marketplace and forced to accept low-paying and unrewarding jobs in order to provide for their families. But work in itself is no guarantee against poverty. 148,000 black female householders worked in managerial or professional jobs in 1979. Of this group, twenty thousand women, or 13.8 percent, still were below the poverty level. Again, this percentage was higher than that for Hispanic professional women (10 percent) and for whites (6.8 percent). Out of 430,000 black women household heads who worked in sales or clerical positions, 106,000, or 24.6 percent, were below the poverty line. 219,000 black women working in private households or as service workers were classified below the poverty level. Three-fourths of all black women farm workers were below the poverty level. The total percentage of black female family heads who held full-time employment and who were below the poverty line (33.2 percent) was higher than the figures for Hispanic women (26.3 percent) and white women (18.9 percent).

The largest categories of black females living in poverty are, as can be expected, the young and the elderly. More black females than males (34.1 percent vs. 27.2 percent) live in poverty. 1,646,000 black females below the age of sixteen years are poor, approximately 41 percent of the total number of black females within this age group (4,012,000). The next age groups that have significant numbers of black women in poverty are between ages sixteen to twenty-one (633,000 females; 36.9 percent of the total age group) and over age sixty-five (489,000 females; 41.7 percent of the total age group). Once more, black females across the board are more likely to be poor than women of other ethnic groups. For example, of white females below the age of sixteen, only 12.2 percent live in poverty. Between the ages of sixteen to twenty-one, 10.5 percent are poor; over age sixty-five, 15.8 percent are poor. Hispanic women are far more likely than whites to be poor at every age level, but without exception are significantly better off than black women. Not surprisingly, black families with female householders are generally deeply in debt. For black families led by females below the poverty line, 213,000 families have an annual income deficit between $1 and $999. 225,000 have annual fiscal deficits between $1000 and $2000; 235,000 families have an annual debt between $2000 and $3000. 197,000 black families headed by females with no husband present sustain annual income shortfalls of $5000 or more. Black families with female heads of household have a mean income deficit that exceeds

$3000 annually, again exceeding the deficits for Hispanic families
($2732) and for whites ($2697). Buried beneath a mountain of bills, it
is little wonder that poor black women are unable to transcend their
impoverishment.

The oppression of black women workers can be illustrated in other
ways beyond the limitations of the poverty line. For example, the median income of a black family with both husband and wife in the work
force is $23,957. For black married couples with only the husband in
the work force, the median income is $17,477. For black female house-
holders where no husband or male is present in the home, the median
family income is only $11,518. This figure is lower than that for white
female household heads ($15,421) and for Hispanic women ($13,330).
The median income for black females over the age of fourteen who
work full-time, regardless of marital status, is $9793. In the Southern
states the income figure is only $8473.

There has been a great deal of rhetoric within black politics about
the impoverishment of the black male at the expense of the black female. Supposedly, black females take jobs away from black males because they are "less threatening" to the system of white male domina-
tion. This line of argument suggests that black women, more than
men, are the chief beneficiaries of affirmative action programs within
the private sector. When one studies the facts, however, one perceives
a radically different picture. First, it is important to isolate the sectors
of black society that are in the upper-income levels. According to 1979
census statistics, there were 9,297,000 white family heads of households who earned $35,000 or more annually. In sharp contrast, only
375,000 black family heads made $35,000 or more. That group
amounts to less than 5 percent of all black family households (4.6 percent). Black family households earning more than $50,000 annually to-
taled 61,000, less than three-fourths of one percent (.73 percent) of all
black family households. Only fourteen thousand black families
earned over $75,000 annually.

Within these upper income groups, black women are severely under-
represented. Four thousand black men and 548,000 white men earned
at least $75,000 in 1979. Fewer than five hundred black women earned
that figure. Fourteen thousand black men earned from $50,000 to
$75,000. Only two thousand black women were in this category. Black
men receiving $35,000 to $50,000 in income numbered 46,000. Only six
thousand black women earned salaries in this range. In 1979, sixty-
eight thousand black males received salaries of $30,000 to $35,000.
About eight thousand black women had this income. In brief, it is an
illusion that black females are achieving at the expense of black males.

The empirical reality is that oppressive conditions exist for black women at every level of the political economy.

President Reagan's proposals for food stamps should have a devastating impact upon poor black women. To understand this fully, we must briefly review the history of the program; what it does, who it helps and why it may be destroyed. The food stamp program was enacted into law almost twenty years ago, and was designed primarily to use up surplus farm products. There were only 425,000 people enrolled in the program in 1964, at a cost of $30 million annually. As late as 1969, only 2.9 million persons were receiving food stamps. It was during the Nixon and Ford Administrations, ironically enough, that the foot stamp program began to grow rapidly. By 1980 there were over twenty-two million Americans on food stamps.

Today, one hears much criticism of food stamp recipients. Ronald Reagan, Jesse Helms and other right-wing politicians tell white America that the program benefits students, the lazy and professional rip-off artists. The realities behind this reactionary rhetoric are radically different. The average food stamp family has an annual income of $3,900. About 90 percent of all food stamp recipients are below the poverty line, which for a family of four is $7,450 per year. Over half have no tangible assets. Fifty-four percent, or over 11.5 million of the recipients of food stamps, are children. Almost 80 percent are unable to work because of age, disabilities or other related reasons. Only 14 percent are adults who are able-bodied and are able to work. Fewer than 1 percent are college or graduate students.

The Reagan Administration's budget includes welfare cuts for pregnant women. According to the Department of Health and Human Services, the new legislation is designed to prohibit states from giving welfare to any pregnant women with no other children, except in the last three months of pregnancy. Thirty-four states now are currently making such payments. Here again, we see that the Reagan budget's assault takes a more aggressive posture against the material interests of women, and particularly against blacks.

Strategies for empowering black women through the legal system and political institutions must become part of a total redefinition of the role of all women within the national political economy. Thus, most of the specific strategies aimed at reducing the forms of oppression against black women must be defined within the general effort to eliminate sexism as a permanent feature of America's economic life and social relations. Legislative reforms along these lines should include the following:

1) *Federal and state legislation should be enacted to create centers for "displaced homemakers."*

Displaced homemakers are women, black and white, who are widowed
or divorced, between the ages of forty-five and sixty-five, and who find
it difficult to obtain work because they have no recent record of paid
employment. Usually they are ineligible for AFDC because their children are generally over eighteen years of age. They cannot receive Social Security because they are not old enough. Since the life expectancy
for black males is approximately sixty years, compared to sixty-nine
for white males and seventy-one for black females, the problem of the
"displaced homemaker" is especially real for black women. One life
insurance study has found that the family income for widows over the
age of fifty-five declines 42 percent. The average policy returns from a
spouse's life insurance plan are generally exhausted within twenty-four
months.

By 1980 sixteen states had adopted displaced homemaker legislation. Recent legislation enacted by the state of Minnesota recognized that "there is an increasing number of persons who, in their
middle years and having fulfilled the role of homemaker, find
themselves displaced because of dissolution of marriage, death of
spouse, or other loss of family income. As a consequence, displaced homemakers have a greatly reduced income, high rate of
unemployment due to age, paid work experience, and discrimination, and limited opportunities to collect funds of assistance from
social security, unemployment compensation, Medicaid and
other health insurance benefits, or pension plans of the spouse."
The Minnesota law created two multipurpose centers for displaced homemakers under the direction of a commissioner of public welfare. The centers counsel women "with respect to appro-
priate job opportunities," provide training and skills necessary
for private or public sector employment, and "refer displaced
homemakers to agencies which may provide information and assistance with respect to health care, financial matters, education,
nutrition, and legal problems."

2) *Federal and state legislation should be enacted to extend labor law protection to domestic or household workers.*

According to a legislative report completed by the New York Bar Association, over 50 percent of all domestic workers are black, and 99 percent are women. The average age of these workers is fifty-one; their
median annual income in 1980 was $2243. Almost half of the nation's
domestic employees are required to work at least fifty weeks every
year. In 1974 the Federal Fair Labor Standards Act granted minimum
wage coverage to domestic employees, but the law has had no practical
impact on the states. The majority of states deny these women work-

ers the right to bargain collectively, and exclude them from the minimum wage level. In the state of New York, "the employers of no more than one-quarter of all household workers contribute to the unemployment insurance fund. Of those workers surveyed by the New York State Household Technicians, approximately one-quarter do not have Social Security."

It is imperative that state labor relations laws be modified to allow domestic employees to create their own unions. Through unionization, domestic workers could be guaranteed certain basic legal rights. The New York Bar Association's legislative report states: "Unionized domestic workers could increase their earnings and obtain such benefits as paid vacations and paid sick leave. Collective bargaining agreements would stabilize work situations by achieving relative uniformity in wages, benefits and working conditions . . . The stigma currently attached to the occupation would be erased and the occupation would be upgraded with increased wages and benefits resulting from concerted activity." In the 1977-78 session, the Connecticut Legislature ratified a measure extending minimum wage laws to domestic workers and empowered the Connecticut Labor Department to enforce this legislation. Unless the federal government moves in this direction, however, the prospects for a worsening of conditions and wages in this sector of the female work force will be accelerated.

3) *Expanded federal programs are needed to create new vocational training opportunities for black, Hispanic and working class white women in traditionally male-dominated sectors of the economy.*

Racial and sexual stereotyping have historically served to perpetuate the lower income status of black women and brown women. A 1975 study of female enrollment in vocational education courses, funded in part by the federal government, reveals a profound race/sex/class bias when the percentage of women in certain programs is scrutinized:

VOCATIONAL COURSE	WOMEN AS PERCENTAGE OF ENROLLEES
Automobile Distributive	4.0
Agriculture	9.4
Technical	11.7
Trades and Industrial	13.4
Petroleum Distributive	14.0
Office	73.5
Health	78.3
Home Economics	83.1
Consumer and Homemaking	84.3

The Vocational Education Act of 1963, amended by the Education Amendments of 1976, created the mandate to "develop and carry out such programs of vocational education within the state, so as to overcome sex discrimination and sex stereotyping in vocational education programs, and thereby furnish equal educational opportunities for persons of both sexes . . ." A sum of $50,000 was granted to each state to hire administrators "to examine all data, plans, grants, procedures and actions with regard to sex discrimination and to assist local agencies in improving educational opportunities for women." Both the national and state advisory councils for vocational education were ordered to select at least one female council member "knowledgeable with respect to the special experiences and problems of sex discrimination in job training and employment . . ." The existing legislation should be expanded to at least include the following provisions: free day care facilities for the children of vocational education students; federal grants and low-interest educational loans to female household heads and homemakers who desire additional skills in order to compete for traditionally "male jobs"; guidance programs aimed at secondary school-level females to reinforce their aspirations and to direct greater numbers of women into certain higher paying vocations; vigorous monitoring of the employment practices of private sector companies holding federal contracts, as well as their policies pertaining to the hiring, promotion and retention of black, Latino and working class white women.

Other federal and state legislation needed to combat sexism and the institutionalization of the lower income conditions of women should involve the expansion of food stamp subsidies (for example, to include all female household heads with one child with annual incomes below $15,000); the adoption of pay equity programs that would reevaluate the salaries of workers in traditionally "women's jobs" and would create a federal mandate to close the wage gap between men and women; and the vigorous prosecution of all agencies, corporations and firms that violate Title VII of the Civil Rights Act of 1964, which forbids unequal payment to employees performing the same work. Such reforms would mark a real beginning in turning the tide against sexism and the continuous war against black and poor women.

The Flight of Capital

In the summer of 1981, the working class of Detroit experienced the highest sustained rate of unemployment since the Great Depression. A cutback in automobile output of 30 percent meant that eighty thousand employees at Chrysler, Ford and General Motors were laid off indefinitely with more expected to follow. Detroit's unemployment rate exceeds 18 percent; for black auto workers the figure is above 25 percent. Black youth unemployment is between 50 to 60 percent and climbing. Similar conditions exist throughout the country. In 1979 the U.S. Department of Labor estimated that over 400,000 workers lost their jobs because of plant closings. Hundreds of thousands more were thrown into unemployment lines because of private industry cutbacks in hiring or reductions in the existing work force short of complete closure.

Americans are accustomed to these kinds of cruel statistics—they no longer surprise us. We live in a society where the system of government and law reflects the rule of private capital. The American Revolution two centuries ago was fought, after all, to liberate one group of domestic entrepreneurs and slaveholders from the unfair restrictions on their right to accumulate and control capital. By capital is meant all forms of private property, money, financial systems, the ownership of the means of production, and distribution of all commodities. All capital in a capitalist society is mobile. Businesses can expand or contract, open and close, or move to any part of the United States—even the world.

Who bears the costs for the high mobility of American capital? Society, of course. First, in order to retain their jobs, most workers must sell their houses, leave friends and family, and relocate to a new environment. All citizens pay for the relocation of a plant in the form of higher state and local taxes whenever a plant departs. The environment also suffers as major businesses relocate periodically in search of lower state and local taxes, nonunion labor, and a generally favorable political climate for capital accumulation. This problem of capital flight was not even perceived as such until some disturbing economic statistics came into public discussion about a decade ago. Familiar American corporate names like General Motors, IBM and General Foods began to conduct more and more of their transactions overseas. The old "mom and pop" neighborhood businesses of the Great Depression and World War II era ultimately gave way to multinational corporations. More foreign capital was invested inside the U.S.; more domestic capital began to move overseas.

An excellent example of the second case is provided by the American banking industry. In 1964 only eleven U.S. banks had overseas branches, and these branch banks held assets totaling only seven billion dollars. In 1972, 107 U.S. banks had foreign branches and assets totaling $90 billion. During this eight year period, Chase Manhattan's share of foreign assets as a portion of total assets increased from 12 to 34 percent. Citibank of New York's percentage rose from 16 to 46 percent. By 1974 the conglomerate owner of Citibank, called Citicorp, earned 62 percent of its total net profits from overseas operations. This capital, for the most part, comes from savings accounts, pension funds and other sources of income derived from our labor. Thus private capital uses American money to finance its own foreign projects that undermine American jobs.

Conservatives in business and politics charge that the crisis of capital flight is no crisis at all, but a liberal-left illusion. According to the research of MIT professor David Birch, who examined the records of a business credit rating service, Dun and Bradstreet, only 2 percent of all private business employment change occurs annually as the direct result of plant closings and relocations. Birch's statistics, like anyone else's, are only as good or accurate as his model of inquiry. Objectively, we know that from 1967 to 1976 the Sunbelt's manufacturing stock grew at roughly twice the rate of that in the Northeast, and 65 percent faster than in the Midwest. We know, by other statistical evidence, that one-sixth of all industrial jobs in New England disappeared between 1969 and 1975. We also know that between 1960 and 1980 there has been a massive shift in the American population from the urban North to the suburban South and West, following the flight of capital. Yet Birch's figure of 2 percent would hardly account for the massive demographic and economic changes that have occurred since 1960. The problem is explained simply by reexamining the question. Professor Birch assessed the behavior of 200,000 firms, which in turn own a total of 5.6 million individual businesses. Of this number only 2 percent closed down, relocated and reopened per year—although usually in the South and West. But does this account for all shifts in capital or property, and not just plant closings *per se*?

How does capital flight occur? Besides the simple closing of a business, factory or plant and its relocation elsewhere, the process includes:

- *The deterioration of existing older facilities.* This is usually caused by not replacing worn-out machines, and using the savings to reinvest in new firms, municipal bonds or other branches of the same firm.

- *Partial capital shift.* This is where some machines, skilled workers, clerical workers and managers are moved to a new area, either in the United States or outside of it. Some "less productive employees" may be laid off, but the old business or plant continues to function at a diminished level of productivity and profitability.

- *Out of state investment.* This happens primarily in the Midwest, New England and Middle Atlantic states. Corporations maintain production levels at the old facility, but take the profits and invest them in new enterprises in the Sunbelt or abroad. In corporate circles, this is a time-honored practice termed "milking." It is politically safe, for it is a virtually invisible form of disinvestment. Workers are often not aware of milking even inside their plants, but it is widespread and economically destructive. For example, in a 1978 poll of the Ohio Manufacturers Association, 70 percent of all corporations in the state spent the majority of their net capital for investment outside of Ohio. In the process of milking, fewer new plants are built in the original location to replace older ones. In major economic recessions, as in 1973-75 and 1980, older industrial states in the Frostbelt are not able to recover as rapidly as Sunbelt states.

● *Exportation of capital.* This happens when banks export their capital and reinvest overseas. Bank laws guarantee the secrecy of all banks' major foreign transactions. One Ohio banker, however, informed the media that the state's major banks had exported $250 million in 1975 alone. The result of such activity is that smaller businesses are unable to compete for bank funds for expansion or even for working capital. Multinational corporations can afford to pay the bill by passing on the cost to the individual consumer; small businesses cannot do so. This forces small producers and distributors out of the marketplace and artificially raises the prices of goods everyone buys.

What is the net result of capital flight from the industrial North and East? The impact is social, cultural, economic, political and racial:

● *Lower corporate taxes.* In 1958, corporations provided 25 percent of the total federal revenue. By 1973 the amount was less than 15 percent. As the average citizen's federal and state tax burden grows, the corporations come closer to getting a free ride.

● *High unemployment.* As American capital finances economic expansion overseas, the amount of capital remaining for business expansion at home contracts. The old rule that "It takes money to make money" still applies. Without sufficient capital investment in manufacturing, thousands of jobs are lost every year. The people who suffer most are those employed in the older industries—especially steel and automobile production. The growing percentage of black and Hispanic workers on the line in both industries means simply that nonwhite laborers will suffer an abnormally high unemployment rate.

● *Population relocation.* Whenever possible, workers follow the flight of jobs. This means that states with right-to-work laws and other statutes that discourage unions will attract capital and thus simultaneously help suppress wages. It is not surprising therefore that the South's total population increased by 15 percent since 1970, and that the West grew by 16 percent. Almost 45 percent of the total U.S. population growth since 1970 has been in only three states—California, Texas and Florida. Meanwhile, the population of Buffalo has declined by 150,000; Washington, D.C. by 200,000; and New York City by almost one million.

• *Fiscal crisis of state and local governments.* When the capital of a community disappears, its tax base contracts. City planners, mayors and state legislators are faced with tough alternatives—either raise new taxes or slash public services. Both choices are fraught with difficulties. Cutting public services such as libraries, schools, sanitation services and fire and police departments means a severe reduction in the quality of cultural and social life for every citizen. The middle class is able to pay for private schools and subsidize its own theatre, cultural arts and so on; the poor cannot. Crime flourishes with the absence of adequate police protection; schools decline; an atmosphere of fear and desperation pervades the social order. On the other hand, raising taxes only accelerates the process. The middle class flees to the suburbs and the poor are left to fend for themselves as best they can. It is a degenerative pattern of human life that can be described at best as cruel. Is it surprising that a permanent underclass of people has emerged in our generation within the major industrial centers—a class with absolutely no prospect of permanent employment, few vocational skills, and little hope for the future?

• *The destruction of small business.* The establishment of any monopoly serves as an inevitable barrier to the development of small enterprise. The multinationals can absorb a small competitor by buying up stock in the company and by hiring key staff at higher salaries. Troublesome firms can be driven out of business by cutting off their access to raw materials, underpricing their products, or by legal and political intimidation. Small businesses cannot afford high-priced legal counsel and generally lack critical marketing and administrative skills. As a result, over three-fourths of all small businesses fail within two years of beginning operations.

In middle-sized, Northern industrial cities, the entrepreneurs hit hardest are inevitably within the black community. According to a

1977 survey of minority-owned businesses conducted by the Department of Commerce, black businessmen in Dayton, Ohio, to cite but one
example, were victims of monopoly in two ways. First, the small entrepreneurs were unable to compete for any significant share of the market—whether in construction, manufacturing, retail or wholesale
trade, real estate or public transport. More importantly, the departure
of major manufacturing firms (National Cash Register, Dayton Tire
and Rubber, etc.) increased the number of black unemployed, blue-
collar workers, thereby decreasing the total purchasing power of black
working-class consumers. Black firms dependent on black consumer
patronage (barbershops, dry cleaners, beauty parlors, neighborhood
grocery stores, etc.) suffered a loss of income. Of 735 black-owned businesses in Dayton, only 18 percent employ at least one paid employee.
394 firms were selected services (beauty parlors, barber shops, etc.);
144 were retail stores; the remainder were small construction companies, insurance firms and taxi cab companies. The average annual gross
receipts for all selected services were only $16,770. The average annual
gross receipts for retail stores without employees were $10,830. The
average annual gross receipts for small manufacturing firms without
employees were $10,330. The total number of workers employed by
black-owned businesses in Dayton during 1977 was 403.

Strategies for limiting the mobility of capital have been effected
with some success in Western European nations, particularly West
Germany and Sweden. In the United States, such a strategy would
have to involve the incremental and gradual transfer of political pre-
rogative from the interests of monopoly capital to the interests of those
who create capital at the point of production—the majority of American working people. A series of "nonreform reforms" designed to create a more productive economic climate for consumers, small businesses and low-to-middle income workers, both black and white, might
include these legislative initiatives:

1) *Tariff codes to discourage the expansion of U.S.-based corporations
   abroad, particularly in such older, heavy industries as steel and auto
   manufacturing.*

2) *Federal legislation to require multinational corporations to pay capital
   gains taxes immediately, and at a higher rate than for firms based only
   in the United States.*

Currently, taxes due on earnings from overseas production can be de-
ferred until the earnings return to the United States. Taxes paid to
foreign governments are deducted from net federal income taxes;
smaller, U.S.-only based firms must consider state and local taxes as a

normal business expense. If federal tax laws were changed to allow smaller domestic businesses to deduct a portion of their state and local taxes from their federal taxes, as well as close tax loopholes for multinationals, major incentives would be created for the expansion of domestic employment.

3) *The creation of a new Reconstruction Finance Corporation, financed by the federal government, which would lend capital to ailing city and state governments, corporations and cooperatives in geographical areas with high unemployment.*

The concept of the Reconstruction Finance Corporation has been revived by urban planner Felix Rohatyn, the chairman of New York City's Municipal Assistance Corporation. Rohatyn's proposal would combine a massive infusion of capital into economically depressed areas with strict wage controls and austere management. The RFC would be capitalized at $5 billion and be allowed to issue up to $25 billion in federally guaranteed bonds to attract foreign and domestic investors. The RFC would then provide no more than 50 percent of the capital to finance any public or private project. Rohatyn also advocates special tax credits for older firms and the expansion of municipal governments' tax bases to include the more affluent suburbs.

The RFC designed by Rohatyn would not substantially reduce black and Hispanic unemployment, nor would it be able to have the fiscal leverage required to generate a capital base within declining urban areas. The RFC proposed here would have to be capitalized at a minimum of $15 billion. Foreign investors would be restricted; bonds purchased by U.S. citizens would be redeemable at a rate sufficiently profitable to attract many of those currently investing in money market funds. Light manufacturing and high technology industries would be ineligible to receive RFC support unless these corporations were located in high unemployment areas. Small, locally-owned businesses would receive long-term, low-interest loans and venture capital. The RFC would encourage the development of consumer and producer cooperatives in the areas of housing, food purchasing, health care, agriculture and other human service related activities. Employees of plants or corporations that were closing or relocating could purchase existing plants with RFC assistance through long-term loans.

4) *Regulation of corporate relocations by local, state and federal agencies.*

The first effort to regulate the relocations of U.S. corporations was the National Employment Priorities Act of 1975 (Ford-Mondale Act). The major features of this unsuccessful legislation were: two-year notification in advance of relocation to the employees and resident population of a community; assistance to businesses to prevent relocations; aid to employees; and loss of tax deferrals on foreign capital gains, etc., if the relocation was not justified. The Ford-Mondale Act was a beginning step toward restricting and regulating capital flight, but, as in the case of Rohatyn's Reconstruction Finance Corporation, the provisions were far too inadequate and overconcentrated at the federal level.

State and local governmental initiatives must be ratified to halt the destruction of jobs. At a minimum, this should involve: a two-year advance notification of the intention to close any plant or firm that employs more than fifty persons in a particular area; community benefits of 25 percent of the gross annual wages of affected employees, paid to a public fund or regional or state RFC which in turn would allocate grant money to depressed communities toward tax loss relief; and a legal requirement that all firms continue to pay employee benefits amounting to two months pay for each year worked.

5) *Intrastate and interstate agreements which would halt the competition for jobs.*

State governors, administrators, mayors and local officials compete against each other for the establishment of businesses in their communities. By attempting to create a favorable corporate climate, officials are coerced into reducing state and local taxes and granting other perks at the fiscal expense of their constituents. State and local governments should resolve to legislate specific forms of competition for private industry, and to halt the practice of "raiding" the Frostbelt states. This legislation would be effective only if Section 14B of the Taft-Hartley Act of 1947, which permits states to outlaw the union shop, is eliminated. This would halt what *Business Week* magazine has termed "The Second War Between the States."

The contemporary crises of America's political economy—the destructive war against black women; sexual and racial discrimination in hiring and vocational mobility; and the loss of jobs in older industrial communities with significant black, brown and lower income populations—cannot be resolved or even abated temporarily through the pursuit of legal remedies of the past. Greater public control of the economy is no longer, as John Maynard Keynes asserted a half century ago, a necessary part of the modern capitalist economic order. That "order" itself is responsible in large measure for the disorder within the lives of millions of working Americans. In short, since large corporations are unable or unwilling to pursue strategies which eliminate racism, sexism and economic stagnation within older urban centers, the American public must involve itself in the democratic challenge of placing its own fiscal house in order.

REFERENCES

Barnet, Richard J. and Muller, Ronald E. *Global Reach: The Power of Multinational Corporations*. New York: Simon and Schuster, 1974.

Beaudry, Ann E., ed. *Women in the Economy: A Legislative Agenda*. Washington, D.C.: Institute for Policy Studies, 1978.

Bluestone, Barry and Harrison, Bennett. *Capital and Communities: The Causes and Consequences of Private Disinvestment*. Washington, D.C.: Progressive Alliance, 1980.

Blumrosen, Ruth G. "Wage Discrimination, Job Discrimination, and Title VII of the Civil Rights Act of 1964." *University of Michigan Journal of Law Reform*, 3(Spring 1979).

Frank, Robert H. and Freeman, Richard T. *The Distributional Consequences of Direct Foreign Investment*. New York: Academic Press, 1978.

Grossman, Allyson S. *Children of Working Mothers, March 1976*. Washington, D.C.: Department of Labor, Bureau of Labor Statistics, 1977.

Grune, Joy Ann, ed. *Manual on Pay Equity: Raising Wages for Women's Work*. Washington, D.C.: Committee on Pay Equity, Conference on Alternative State and Local Policies, 1980.

Harrison, Bennett and Hill, Edward. *The Changing Structure of Jobs in Older and Younger Cities*, New England Political Economy Working Paper Number 2. Cambridge, Mass.: Joint Center for Urban Studies, MIT and Harvard University, October 1978.

Hutner, Frances C. *Economic Role of Women*. New York: Joint Council on Economic Education, 1977.

Kelly, C. Edward. *Industrial Exodus: Public Strategies for Control of Corporate Relocation*. Washington, D.C.: Conference/Alternative State and Local Public Policies, 1977.

Lerner, Jane; Bergstrom, Fredell; and Champagne, Joseph. *EVE: Equal Vocational Education*. Houston: 1976.

Mick, Stephan. "Social and Personal Costs of Plant Shutdowns." *Industrial Relations*, 14(May, 1975).

Perry, David and Watkins, Alfred, eds. *The Rise of the Sunbelt Cities,* Urban Affairs Annual Reviews, No. 14. Beverly Hills, Cal.: Sage Publications, 1978.

Ratner, Ronnie. *Equal Employment Policy for Women: Strategies for Implementation in the United States, Canada, and Western Europe.* Wesleyan, Mass.: Temple University Press, 1979.

Rowen, James. "Public Control of Public Money." *The Progressive Magazine,* (February 1977).

Sale, Kirkpatrick. *Power Shift: The Rise of the Southern Rim and Its Challenge to the Eastern Establishment.* New York: Random House, 1975.

Schweke, William, ed. *Plant Closings: Issues, Politics, and Legislation.* Washington, D.C.: Economic Development Project, Conference on Alternative State and Local Policies, 1980.

Smith, David and McGuigan, Patrick. *The Public Balance Sheet: Calculating the Costs and Benefits of Community Stabilization.* Washington, D.C.: Conference on Alternative State and Local Policies, 1979.

Smith, Lee. "The EEOC's Bold Foray Into Job Evaluation." *Fortune Magazine,* (September 11, 1978).

Steiger, JoAnn and Cooper, Sara. *Vocational Preparation of Women: A Report of the Secretary's Advisory Committee on the Rights and Responsibilities of Women.* Washington, D.C.: U.S. Government Printing Office, 1976.

United States Bureau of the Census, Department of Commerce. *The Social and Economic Status of the Black Population in the United States: An Historical View, 1790-1978.* Washington, D.C.: U.S. Government Printing Office, 1980, Second Printing.

United States Department of Labor Women's Bureau. *The Legal Status of Homemakers in Each State.* Washington, D.C.: U.S. Government Printing Office, 1979.

WHITE ETHNIC NEIGHBORHOODS AND THE SOCIAL GOOD

Richard J. Krickus

Mary Washington College

Introduction

By the mid-1970s, the urban policymaking community—planners, journalists, private consultants, public administrators, elected officials, etc.—had discovered neighborhoods. Since then, conferences conducted by social scientists have devoted workshops, panels and colloquia to "neighborhood stabilization," "community organization," and other issues bearing on neighborhoods. Influential members of the legislative and executive branches at both ends of Pennsylvania Avenue celebrated neighborhood revitalization as essential to the restoration of our older cities. During the 1976 presidential campaign and after he took office, Jimmy Carter stated that neighborhoods would be a central part of his urban strategy. Toward this end he chose Robert Embrey, formerly Baltimore's housing commissioner, and Geno Baroni, an articulate national exponent of community development, to work for him at the Department of Housing and Urban Development. Congress, however, refused to enact such legislation which would underpin Carter's urban strategy as, for example, his proposal for a National Development Bank and a bill providing states with incentives to become more deeply involved in solving urban problems.

One does not hear and read as much about neighborhoods today as several years ago, but urban policymakers continue to sing their praises. They often display a special affection for ethnic neighborhoods because they provide our cities with the "diversity all city lovers cherish." Nonetheless, their rhetoric aside, most urban policymakers do not appreciate the value of neighborhoods to cities, and in the case of white ethnic neighborhoods, many urban analysts believe (lapsing into a favorite Sixties' aphorism) that they are "part of the problem, not part of the solution." The neglect of neighborhoods, and hostile reactions to white ethnic neighborhoods in particular, stems from a host of circumstances:

(1)   Unlike families and corporations, neighborhoods have no legal status and cannot resort to the legal system for self protection.

(2)   Although many neighborhoods are larger than municipalities, they have no governmental powers such as zoning or the ability to float bonds that would allow them to control their fiscal destiny.

(3)   Although planners speak about plugging social variables into their schema, most cling to a physical bias, reflecting the architectural and engineering origins of their profession. Hence, a slum is defined in terms of physical deterioration when the principal feature of a slum is social disorganization—family fragmentation, high rates of crime, the absence of viable community institutions, etc.

(4)   There is pervasive ignorance about ethnicity in our society, and a normative bias that it is pernicious. Both Western and Marxist social theory, for example, claim that ethnicity, a "relic" of an earlier, premodern era, declines in the face of urbanization, industrialization, and other features of modern life. Ethnic values and ties which have survived the crucible of modernization are the source of intergroup discord and are the basis for particularistic behavior inimical to the acceptance of universal norms. Marxists claim that ethnicity is a reactionary impulse which undermines the formation of an international proletarian consciousness. Western humanists argue that it has been responsible for two world wars in this century alone. Under these circumstances, it is not surprising that American policymakers adhere to empirical and normative assumptions ill-disposing them to assess the ethnic factor in a balanced fashion.

(5)   It is conventional wisdom that those white ethnic neighborhoods remaining in the city are rapidly declining; it is, therefore, senseless to single them out for special attention.

(6)   Many commentators assert that those white ethnic neighborhoods which have survived rapid social change are bastions of racism.

It has been against this backdrop of legal and governmental limitations on the one hand, and intellectual confusion and empirical half-truths on the other, that policymakers have adopted policies which have expedited the decline of neighborhoods in our older cities. The purpose of this essay is to demonstrate why neighborhoods are so critical to the vitality of our cities, and to show that they contribute to the welfare of everybody living in the metropolis. Much of the discussion pertains to viable black and Hispanic neighborhoods, but the author will focus upon white ethnic neighborhoods, which he knows best.[1]

The Rise and Decline of White Ethnic Neighborhoods

In the late 19th and early 20th centuries, the lure of jobs drew most of the second-wave European immigrants (largely from Eastern and Southern Europe) to particular locales in the United States. Jews were attracted to the garment industry in New York City, Poles to the coal mines of Pennsylvania, and Lithuanians to the stockyards of Chicago. One of the largest Hungarian neighborhoods in the United States developed in East Toledo when, at the turn of the century, the British-owned National Malleable Castings Company built a steel plant along the Maumee River. Hungarian immigrants who worked for the firm in Cleveland were transported to serve as the backbone of the Toledo plant's work force. Subsequently, friends and relatives from the "old country" arrived, found jobs in the mill and other plants in the area, and settled in East Toledo's Birmingham section, which acquired its name from its British benefactors.

Over time, immigrant settlements took on a distinctive character reflecting the confluence of old and new world values, experiences and institutions. In many instances the formation of an ethnic parish (where Mass was conducted in Polish, Lithuanian or Hungarian), along with a parochial school and convent, was the foundation upon which an ethnic neighborhood was built. After World War I, the largest Polish parish in the United States, St. Stanislaw Kostka in Chicago, was home for 140 organizations—mutual aid societies, women's organizations, youth groups, cultural associations, and various other organizations serving the parish's Polish immigrants.[2]

In the case of other immigrant communities the church was less of a cohesive factor; for example, tight-knit kinship networks along with village and fraternal organizations gave impetus to "Little Italies" in America. First formed at the turn of the century, Italian-American neighborhoods today thrive in many cities in the North and East because the residents highly value the Italian-American lifestyle associated with them.

Lest we contribute to the conventional view that ethnic neighborhoods are always places where a single ethnic group resides, we should stress that at least four kinds of ethnic neighborhoods have been a vital part of urban America in the 20th century.

Ethnically Homogeneous Neighborhoods

Because of lingual, cultural and ethno-religious affinities, most immigrants preferred to live among their "own kind." This accounts for the existence of ethnically homogeneous neighborhoods in large cities like Boston, New York and Chicago, as well as in smaller ones like Gary, Indiana, and McKees Rocks, Pennsylvania.

Ethnically Mixed Neighborhoods: Largely Segregated

Another kind of white ethnic neighborhood, perhaps the most common one, comprises two or more ethnic groups. In the first half of this century, the Ironbound section of Newark was home for Germans, Jews, Italians and other immigrants, and although some of them lived there randomly, ethnic segregation was the norm in other areas of the neighborhood.

Ethnically Mixed Neighborhood: Largely Integrated

A third type of white ethnic neighborhood involves the presence of many ethnic groups with little or no segregation. The residents of the "old neighborhood" leave it to live in a "better" part of town, or one closer to their place of employment. People who formerly lived in Ironbound, for example, relocated in the Clinton Hill and Vailsburg sections of Newark beginning in the 1930s.

Ethnic Neighborhoods and Communities in the Suburbs

It is generally believed that suburbanization spells the end of the ethnic factor as an important element in the lives of white ethnic Americans. This conclusion is premature because: (a) many suburbs house a single ethnic group—Poles in Warren, Michigan, and Italians in Lodi, New Jersey; (b) other areas, though comprising several ethnic groups, are ethnically segregated—parts of Long Island for example; and (c) even in the ethnically heterogeneous suburbs, ethnic communities have survived the dispersion of their groups' members through social networks. People may have to travel great distances, yet social life revolves around the parish, the family and ethnic organizations and clubs. One can find such communities in metropolitan areas of the Great Lakes region, New England and the Mid-Atlantic states.

There is no question, however, that suburbanization has contributed to the decline of numerous white ethnic neighborhoods. After World War II, millions of those who lived in them sought a better quality of life in the suburbs—a single family detached home, a two-car garage, open space, less traffic congestion, and a respite from street crime. But although market forces contributed to this out-migration, many federal urban programs designed to revitalize our older cities expedited this trend by destroying central city residential communities. One of the first analysts to point this out was Martin Anderson in *The Federal Bulldozer*.[3] He was formerly President Reagan's chief domestic affairs advisor.

Because of his avowed conservativism, liberals rejected Anderson's charges for many years. Believing in the capacity of government to solve most of society's problems, they deemed such charges as slander, calculated to destroy public confidence in positive government. But today few analysts, whatever their political convictions, deny that federal housing, transportation and redevelopment programs have been the source of many urban problems—the concentration of blacks in older cities and the destruction of viable neighborhoods to name just two of them.

Up until the early 1960s, Federal Housing Administration and Veterans Administration officials adopted policies that fostered racial segregation in metropolitan areas. They discouraged whites from purchasing homes in the city, encouraging them instead to buy homes in the suburbs. Conversely, they steered prospective black homeowners away from the suburbs toward the city. This practice, along with *de jure* and later *de facto* racial covenants, blockbusting and disinvestment, resulted in a dual migration—the flight of whites from the cities and of blacks and Hispanics into them.

Even after such discriminatory practices were halted, federally supported programs contributed to racial segregation. In many cities white ethnic neighborhoods were severed by construction of inner-city expressways. This ultimately gave rise to the out-migration of the neighborhood's remaining residents. People whose homes and businesses had been spared left because the community's integrity had been devastated. Contrary to a belief popular among urbanologists, this phenomenon often did not benefit house-hungry minority people who moved into the area. Because the previous homeowners and landlords had not kept up their dwellings once they discovered their neighborhood had been marked for "renewal," the newcomers found a deteriorating housing inventory. Because they were poor or near-poor, little mortgage or rehabilitation money was made available to them or to their landlords, and over time the number of abandoned dwellings mushroomed. What had once been a viable neighborhood became an urban wasteland or a concentration point for the city's neediest residents.

Due to the effects of urban renewal programs, many white ethnic neighborhoods were destroyed on a wholesale basis.[4] Often they were never redeveloped; if they were, few low-income homes were included in the package. This contributed to already badly overcrowded conditions for minority residents. As one observer has written:

> Conceived by some of its original Congressional sponsors as a way of building better housing for slum dwellers, urban renewal instead became what the real estate industry and industry wanted: a generous federal subsidy for the development of high-profit complexes of offices, luxury apartments, and grand civic improvements in or adjacent to local business centers.[5]

Setting aside the political and economic forces which explain why urban renewal was employed in this manner, many urban policymakers just do not appreciate the importance of social systems to the metropolitan area. They employ only physical criteria in defining slums, and this means that neighborhoods with old but sound dwellings, and stable families and community institutions, are deemed ripe for the bulldozer.

The most popular urban redevelopment strategy involves the central business district, or CBD. City planners are trained to manipulate the physical environment to maximize the urban system's economic capacity. Consequently, the typical downtown restoration strategy has been to restore the CBD to its former prominence and to expand the commercial and tax-producing properties in or near it. Insofar as restoring downtown is a necessary part of reclaiming it from spreading urban blight and economic decline, the strategy cannot be faulted. The restoration of Baltimore's harbor district, involving a complex of restaurants, quality fast food outlets and shops, has been a success. The problem with the CBD strategy, however, is twofold. First, it often is the only restoration strategy adopted, so all but a small percentage of redevelopment funds are invested in it, leaving residential communities starving for capital. Second, in order to make room for the complex or to facilitate traffic to and from it, viable neighborhoods mistakenly defined as gray areas "soon to be slums" are destroyed. Armed with physical criteria and an aesthetic sensibility hostile to urban neighborhoods, planners write off white ethnic neighborhoods marked by old housing, high density and mixed land use. The businesses, homes, churches and factories are considered expendable for expressway construction or renewal. Predictably, what once was a healthy neighborhood, with strong families, profitable small business strips and viable local institutions, becomes a slum after a significant number of dwellings are flattened. The people who survive the clearing operation soon leave because they know that from there the neighborhood can only go downhill.

By the time Jimmy Carter entered office, there were few liberals who disputed the allegation that misguided federal programs contributed to the demise of healthy neighborhoods. But today, the Reagan Administration and conservatives must acknowledge that actions taken by private interests are also contributing to their destruction. First, blockbusting and disinvestment (the refusal of lending institutions to make loans available or of insurance companies to write policies in red-lined neighborhoods) have contributed to the decline of many urban residential communities.[6] Second, it is clear that many federal programs have not achieved the objectives Congress intended because powerful private interests have had a virtual veto over them.[7]

Of course, private entrepreneurs are not obligated to invest in ventures which do not meet with their approval—but this is not the issue. Rather, the crux of the matter is that when private interests are involved in public endeavors, they must accept the ground rules— namely, private firms should receive a fair return on their investments, but the public interest must be served in the process. This clearly was not true of the urban renewal program, which was originally designed to construct residential dwellings, a significant proportion of which were earmarked for low-income residents. It became instead a program that was employed for other uses, often at the expense of minority groups and many white ethnic residents as well.

Nothing can be done about neighborhoods which already have been destroyed, but as we design new urban reclamation strategies in the 1980s—whether they be private, public, or a combination of both—it is clear that the preservation of viable residential communities must be an integral part of them.

White Ethnic Neighborhoods Today

It is undeniable that many white neighborhoods have disappeared from cities where they once thrived. This accounts for the claim that they are of secondary importance to most cities and it therefore is much more sensible to concentrate on downtown revitalization. The simple truth, however, is that many white ethnic neighborhoods still can be found in our Northeastern and Midwestern industrial cities; indeed, most of the whites living in these cities are the children or grandchildren of the people who comprised the second wave of European immigration. The number of people involved runs into the millions.

The residents of these neighborhoods have endured problems which have driven whites and middle-class blacks to the suburbs. A large number of homes are owner-occupied; social life revolves around the parish, the family and ethnic organizations; and small businesses still thrive. Employing the typology outlined earlier, there is good reason to believe that ethnicity is a critical variable in explaining why some white neighborhoods have survived while others have disappeared. Those fitting the "ethnically homogeneous" and "ethnically mixed: largely segregated" categories seem to have survived the disruption associated with rapid social change better than neighborhoods where ethnic ties were weak. This seems to explain why in some of the nation's most troubled cities—Newark, Detroit and Cleveland—the "Little Italies" still remain intact.[8]

White ethnics who have refused to join the white flight to the suburbs, however, have not been congratulated for remaining in the old neighborhood; on the contrary, they have been accused of racism for wishing to maintain the ethnic character of their communities. Because white and black central-city residents live in urban pressure-cookers, racial tensions are a fact of life. But those commentators who conclude that racism is the primary reason for the existence of white ethnic neighborhoods in cities with large minority populations ignore three important facts. First, most existing white ethnic neighborhoods were formed generations before a significant number of blacks and Hispanics migrated to the nation's Frostbelt cities. Second, many residents of white ethnic neighborhoods continue to reside in them primarily because they want to live among people who share a common subculture; their motives are positive—not negative. Paul Wrobel, an anthropologist who studied St. Thaddeus Parish (in a Polish neighborhood in Detroit), discussed this accusation with a resident, Maggie Krajewski. She said:

> Everybody calls us racist, just because we want to live in a Polish-American neighborhood. I'm sick and tired of hearing all these educated people telling the rest of us how we should live, especially those limousine liberals who live in Grosse Pointe or West Bloomfield, or the middle-class blacks who live in the city and send their kids to private schools. Hell no, I don't mind if a black family moves in next door or across the street. Right now there are four black families on our street and there ain't no problems for anyone. They even send their kids to St. Thaddeus school. But when you ask me if I would be happy with a majority of blacks in the neighborhood, I would have to say no. Go ahead, call me a racist. I don't give a damn. The reason I feel like I do is this: if we had a majority of blacks, then this neighborhood wouldn't be the same anymore. It wouldn't be a Polish neighborhood. Is there something wrong with me feeling that way?[9]

Few Americans who trace their ancestry to the "second wave" of European immigration think of themselves as "white ethnics," and when employing hyphenated terms like Polish- or Italian-American, they stress the word "American." The ethnic factor is not as important in shaping the thoughts and actions of Americans as in the case of the Basques in Spain, the Lithuanians in the USSR or the Ibo in Nigeria, but even when factors such as education, income and occupational status are controlled in surveys, white ethnics express thoughts and behave in a manner different from similarly situated Americans on a range of social, economic and political matters. The differences may not be dramatic, but they exist because of the shaping influence of common ethnic values and experiences.[10] As Harold Isaacs has written, an ethnic group's language, culture and shared historical experiences, the components of what he calls "basic group identity," are vital to the psychic and social well-being of its members. An individual's identity, the formation of his personality, and the values which give meaning to his life are shaped by group affinities, religious beliefs and other phenomena which social theorists have labelled "premodern."[11] Even though it is a grave intellectual error to infer that the ethnic factor is as critical to the behavior of white ethnics in America as it is to the aforementioned groups, it is surely shortsighted to study American society and dismiss ethnicity altogether.

Finally, in many cities in the Northeast and Midwest the only integrated neighborhoods are those which are primarily inhabited by white ethnics. To cite just one example, in Newark's North Ward there are 100,000 residents: 60 percent are white, mostly Italian-American; 25 percent are Hispanic, largely Puerto Rican; and 15 percent are black. Some areas of the ward are integrated, whereas in other areas minority residents live along its outer boundaries. Minority residents choose to reside in the North Ward because the white residents are strongly attached to it; homeowners and landlords keep their dwellings in good condition, and residents can shop in neighborhood stores, send their children to parochial schools (an important consideration to many black and Puerto Rican parents), and walk the streets in greater safety than in other areas of the city. Much the same situation exists in parts of Baltimore, Cleveland and Philadelphia, where white ethnic residents and institutions have survived spreading urban blight and social disorganization. The common bond of shared ethnic values and ties is the single most important reason for their choosing to remain in the city. Moreover, in the 1970s, many efforts to organize such neighborhoods for community action were successful because the residents shared a common ethnic bond.

White Ethnic Neighborhoods, the Social Good and Public Policy

Most Americans accept the proposition that wetlands and forests must be preserved because their destruction diminishes the quality of life not only for flora and fauna living in or near them, but for every living thing in the ecological system as well. The same holds true for neighborhoods, which are as vital to the quality of life in our cities and suburbs as wetlands are to the ecological system, for their destruction touches the lives of everyone residing in the metropolis. With their decline a host of grim consequences is set into motion:

* Neighborhoods bonded by a sense of community, of sharing and caring, are lost, along with jobs, business revenues and property taxes, denying local jurisdictions the funds needed to provide services to disadvantaged residents who cannot relocate elsewhere.

* In areas where they serve as buffer zones "protecting" more affluent communities from "urban blight," middle-class residents often flee to the suburbs, or in those instances where close-in suburbs are "exposed," they strike out for even more distant parts of the metropolis.

* An environment of despair develops, causing industry, retail businesses and residents who may be far from the "war zone" to leave "because the city has no future."

* For all of the preceding reasons, public and private reclamation programs in the pipeline or under consideration are put in jeopardy, often making certain that funds for housing, education, health and other vital needs will be wasted, poorly utilized, or only serve as temporary solutions to deep-seated problems.

Economic changes dictate that many Frostbelt cities no longer can provide job opportunities for their residents. This will necessitate a population decline and, unfortunately, the eventual demise of viable neighborhoods. If we are to save as many as possible, and keep from repeating this pattern in newer areas, it is imperative that policymakers at all levels of government develop a sophisticated understanding of what impact their policies will have upon residential communities. Because federal policymakers have been negligent along these lines, they are responsible for an appalling contradiction: billions of dollars have been allocated for community development while at the same time, through neglect, ignorance and greed, hundreds of neighborhoods that once sustained healthy families, profitable businesses and viable local institutions have been destroyed. Local political authorities must recognize that by allowing residents to have a voice in policies affecting their neighborhoods, the interests of everybody living in the city can be enhanced. The following example is illustrative.

For years the residents of the largely Hungarian-American neighborhood of Birmingham had urged the city fathers of East Toledo to build an overpass to facilitate traffic over railroad tracks dividing the neighborhood. The authorities refused to comply until the early 1970s when suburban development adjacent to Birmingham created traffic bottlenecks. The planners, however, insisted the overpass be four lanes; this would require widening the neighborhood's major street, Consaul Street. Several churches, along with a substantial number of homes and businesses, would be destroyed. Only after residents, several hundred strong, marched on city hall did the authorities agree to an alternative plan.

The decision to build the overpass and make Consaul Street a four-lane street made sense to the city's engineers, but illustrated their ignorance about the importance of neighborhoods to a city. Their original plan would have destroyed the community's main street, an action eventually leading to the neighborhood's decline. The site recommended by the residents and finally adopted by the city was in Ironville, one of the first urban renewal projects undertaken by Toledo. Typically, after the old neighborhood had been bulldozed and new streets and sewer lines constructed, a significant proportion of the cleared land was never developed.

The new site meant that the alternative route had to be one-tenth of a mile longer, the overpass itself had to be twice as long as the original one, and the cost of the project was somewhat higher—but not one home or business would be destroyed. This was where the construction should have been planned in the first place. Even accepting the city's economic criteria, the alternative route made more sense than the original one, which was predicated upon the virtual destruction of Birmingham.

Urban analysts are fond of referring to the city as a system comprised of many interrelated parts—economic, physical, political and social. The stark truth, though, is that few of them adopt measures which are systemic in nature. In some instances overriding political or economic considerations explain this oversight, but in other cases the problem is an intellectual one. We have already mentioned this condition but need to stress it because generally people who think of themselves as hard-nosed realists do not understand the economic advantages associated with stable social systems. In a word, stable neighborhoods provide a host of services free—the care of young and old people, the amelioration of anti-social behavior, etc.—but once the neighborhoods are seriously disrupted these same services must be paid for out of public revenues and delivered by public agencies. The preservation of neighborhoods, therefore, should be a major goal of the Reagan Administration, which is ostensibly committed to smaller government and the principle of voluntarism.

Notwithstanding the fact that white ethnic neighborhoods are declining, policymakers should determine how the most recent wave of immigration to urban America might have a bearing on neighborhood revitalization. In the aftermath of World War II, many white ethnic neighborhoods on the decline were given a boost when displaced persons moved in. Today, immigrants who first arrived here in the 1970s may serve a similar purpose. For example, because of the presence of approximately 50,000 Russian Jews, the Brighton Beach area of Brooklyn once again is a thriving neighborhood. Not too far away in Newark, Portuguese migrants have contributed to the revitalization of Ironbound, prompting observers there to speak of "Portuguese renewal."

The New York metropolitan area has been inundated by immigrants from every corner of the globe in the last ten years. Bishop Anthony J. Bevilacqua, using government figures, estimates that in Brooklyn and Queens alone there are, in addition to the Russian Jews, 700,000 Spanish-speaking people, 200,000 Greeks, 175,000 Italians, 140,000 Haitians, 100,000 Chinese, 100,000 West Indians, 75,000 Koreans, 75,000 Poles, 50,000 Filipinos, 40,000 Croatians, 20,000 East Asians, 6,000 Portuguese and 3,000 Czechs.[12]

Looking at the nation at large, one observes that in the four regions of the country deserving of the label "megalopolis," various ethnic groups make up a significant portion of the population. In addition to the megalopolis running from Southern New Hampshire to Northern Virginia, we find one winding along the southern shore of the Great Lakes, another running from San Francisco to the Mexican border, and still another developing up the east coast of the Florida peninsula. In designing plans to control growth in these regions, planners would be remiss not to explore how ethnicity may have a bearing on their schemes.

Finally, in light of the Reagan Administration's commitment to block-grants, the states will play a larger role in urban affairs in the 1980s than they have in the recent past. It is imperative that the states develop neighborhood stabilization and revitalization programs and appreciate how urban neighborhoods can enhance their ability to meet the housing needs of their citizens. Many states may find it is less expensive to provide housing in cities than in the suburbs or rural areas. In 1975, then HUD Secretary Carla A. Hills, speaking before a gathering of the National League of Cities, said, "We know it takes almost 50 percent less of everything—land, labor, and environmental disruption—to rehabilitate a city neighborhood."[13] Stricken with stagflation and cutbacks in federal assistance (an estimated 25 percent, but with inflation the amount is closer to 37 percent), states should keep in mind that many cities have thousands of sound dwellings which, because of inflation, are now economically feasible to rehabilitate. Also, in contrast to open areas outside of the cities, sewer, water and electrical lines are already in place, and thus do not have to be constructed anew.

In addition to physical assets, the states should exploit the social infrastructures existing in white ethnic neighborhoods, making them attractive places to live for newcomers as well as for the current residents. Because they are anchor points in many cities, centers of stability in the midst of rapid change, the prospects of reclaiming the adjacent urban wastelands are vastly improved.

For all of the preceding reasons, it is imperative that policymakers begin to perceive ethnicity as an asset to a city, not as a problem or limitation, and, by their actions, acknowledge that white ethnic neighborhoods are a social good.

NOTES

[1] Unless otherwise indicated, the data and analysis presented rest heavily upon culling in-house reports generated by the staff at the National Center for Urban Ethnic Affairs and interviews with neighborhood activists such as Don Eschelman and Steve Adubato of Newark, Peter Ujvagi of Toledo, and Joe McNeeley of Baltimore.

[2] Richard J. Krickus, *Pursuing the American Dream* (New York: Anchor Books, 1976).

[3] Martin Anderson, *The Federal Bulldozer: A Critical Analysis of Urban Renewal, 1949-1962* (Cambridge, Mass.: MIT Press, 1964).

[4] Blacks, of course, were affected too, but unlike their white counterparts, most of them could find alternative housing only in the city.

[5] Leonard Downie, *Mortgage on America* (New York: Praeger Books, 1974), p. 62.

[6] The National Commission on Neighborhoods, *People Building Neighborhoods* (Washington, D.C.: Government Printing Office, 1979), pp.. 86-117.

[7] In addition to Downie, op. cit., see also Harold Kaplan, *Urban Renewal Politics* (New York: Columbia University Press, 1963).

[8] This matter has not received the attention it deserves. Further research might indicate that ethnicity *per se* is not the major factor, but rather that specific ethnic groups are more attached to their neighborhoods than other ones—the Italians, for example, in contrast to the Hungarians or the Lithuanians. Economic, social and political factors unique to a specific city or metro-

politan area may account for the survival of some ethnic neighborhoods, while others have faded from the scene.

⁹ Paul Wrobel, *Our Way* (South Bend, Ind.: Notre Dame Press, 1979).

¹⁰ Mary Ann Krickus, "The Status of East European Women in the Family: Tradition and Change," *Conference on the Educational and Occupational Needs of White Ethnic Women* (Washington, D.C.: The National Institute of Education, 1980).

¹¹ Harold Isaacs, *Idols of the Tribe* (New York: Harper and Row, 1975), pp. 135-136.

¹² *The Washington Star* (May 18, 1981).

¹³ *The Washington Post* (December 4, 1975).

NEIGHBORHOOD SEGREGATION BY RACE AND CLASS: AN AMERICAN TRADITION

Peter J. Kellogg

University of Wisconsin-Green Bay

During the 1960s and 1970s, the American public developed a dramatic new awareness of the existence of racial and ethnic groups. Civil rights protest seemed to produce both a Black Power movement and a white ethnic backlash. People feared clashes of hard hats with black militants and the fragmentation or polarization of the society around newly articulated ethnic concerns. White ethnic groups and blacks seemed to be verging on violent conflict over housing, jobs and schools. Politicians fanned the discontents in efforts to use "the social issue" to gain votes, hoping to turn white ethnic groups against black Americans and their allies, or called for "benign neglect" of racial issues to avoid further polarization. Ethnicity and the conflicts that seemed to swirl around it became a center of controversy, one side advocating a return to historic ethnic roots, another fearing that such group identification would rend the society, and others cynically trying to exploit the tensions. As the courts began to order busing for school desegregation in a desperate effort to overcome the racial isolation that stemmed from segregated housing patterns in cities, neighborhood integrity and ethnic purity suddenly became rallying cries. Racial justice and ethnic integrity were seen as opposing forces, as conflicting moral imperatives.

One of the results of these controversies has been a growing body of scholarship and polemic analysis which defends the white ethnic experience in America. These defenses have often been angry and shrill, usually attacking white liberals and government bureaucrats for ignoring white ethnic groups or holding them in contempt. Efforts to deal with racism and black poverty have been pictured as misguided or even deliberately destructive of ethnic groups. Andrew Greeley, for example, wrote that:

> Busing is a deliberate, self-conscious, and explicit attempt to destroy the neighborhood school because it is, in principle, racist.

Indeed, in principle, neighborhoods are racist, and if you manage
to destroy the neighborhood school, sure enough, the neighborhood itself soon begins to crumble. Which of course proves ex-
actly what the pro-busing forces want to prove: people who live
in the neighborhood are racists.[1]

One of the main concerns of these ethnic defenders has been that the
achievements and aspirations of white ethnic groups have been forgotten. The needs of white ethnics, they believe, have been ignored as
society rushed to undo centuries of injustice to black Americans. On
one level, this scholarship has been a call for the understanding of ethnic groups and the expansion of government policy to meet more of
their needs. On another level, however, the writing has shown an implicit jealousy of, or hostility to, black people and black struggles. The
ethnic defenders' blanket attacks on liberals and government programs
have very likely contributed to the current dismantling of the social
welfare programs of the sixties, a process which seems about to undo
most of the redistributive gains of that decade, modest as they were.
The defense of white ethnics may have contributed to a reaction that
could prove disastrous to the poor and working class of all groups.

Undoubtedly, the champions of the white ethnic experience are
making a vital contribution. The history of popular attitudes toward
successive waves of European immigrants and their descendants is a
tragic litany of oppression and humiliation. Immigration was re-
stricted and immigrant culture suppressed. The dignity and achievement of those peoples surely deserve far more recognition and support
than they have received previously. The struggle for white ethnic
pride seems as justified as the struggle for black pride. Pluralism has
been generally successful with respect to religions and should be
equally valued with respect to ethnic cultures. Pride seems far less
divisive than any effort to scorn or suppress the ethnic heritages which
have been an integral part of the histories and identities of many people. Clearly, it was unfair and dangerous to picture only Southern
"rednecks" and Northern ethnics as the archetypical racists, but that
was done, to the satisfaction of the likes of George Wallace and Kevin
Phillips with their cynical calculations for the political exploitation of
the resulting resentments. The scholarly defenders of ethnicity have
performed an important service in bringing the claims and the history
of white ethnic groups into greater public consciousness. At the same
time, these ethnic defenders have often minimized deeper issues involved in the emerging racial conflicts and have made the solution of
those conflicts more difficult.

I wish to argue that the emphasis on conflicts between the claims of
race and ethnicity has tended to obscure more basic issues of class and

democracy which must be addressed before the problems of either Afro-Americans or white ethnic groups can be resolved. Racial and ethnic groups should be united in coalitions fighting to advance their many common interests, and should not jealously fight each other over crumbs of status or economic advantage. Exploring the relationship between race, class, ethnicity and neighborhood provides a fruitful approach to these larger issues which shape not only the structure and needs of neighborhoods, but many other fundamental social questions as well. The ethnic defenders may well score valid points against the liberals for ignoring legitimate and pressing ethnic needs, but the problem with liberals is not that they advocate too much government involvement, but too little, or, as Richard Krickus points out, that they cannot keep business interests from dominating and perverting government efforts.[2] Black and ethnic Americans have similar histories and similar needs—though Afro-Americans have suffered exclusion of a far more pervasive and crushing kind—and they are natural allies both in their need for cultural vindication and in their shared experience of exclusion and exploitation. The ethnics do need to be defended, not against black Americans or even liberals, but against the continuing injustice of the inequitable distribution of income, wealth and power in America.

Despite the furor and even violence over busing for desegregation, the major historic conflicts between blacks and white ethnics have been over housing and neighborhoods. Memphis' vindication of its policy of blocking off streets connecting black and white neighborhoods is only the latest example of a conflict that has been taking place for generations. By tracing the history of housing and neighborhoods in American cities, it is possible to show the salience of class and demonstrate that emphasizing the racial and ethnic dimensions of the conflict masks the underlying issues. The history of neighborhood conflict, neglect, decay and transformation graphically illustrates the fundamental class nature of the problems and the process by which class issues have been obscured by racial and ethnic divisions. American cities have been historically segregated—by class as well as by race. For generations ethnic groups as well as black people have been the victims of this segregation, although upward mobility, especially since World War II, has begun to give many white ethnics real or apparent freedom from such exclusion. Throughout their history American cities have been systematically segregated by class, and during most of the twentieth century that segregation has been formally and legally supported by a variety of governmental policies.

When walking was the main form of urban transportation, the well-to-do lived near the center of the city and the central business district, while the poor and the working class were concentrated in the urban fringe. As other forms of transportation developed, particularly during the mid-nineteenth century, urban residential patterns began to change as the affluent moved to the first dormitory suburbs and the poor began to inherit their older homes near the center city. The flux and uncertainty of that period caused great tensions as the middle class sought to secure an economically homogeneous environment amidst the turbulence of cities rapidly growing and experiencing the migration of diverse groups of poor. An urban historian describes the situation as producing an urban crisis from which the middle class was to flee to the suburbs:

> The combination of high population mobility, widespread eco-
> nomic insecurity, and class, ethnic, racial, and neighborhood ten-
> sions constituted the major elements out of which the mid-nine-
> teenth century urban crisis emerged. As the blighted fringe
> expanded, pushing waves of poverty, disease, and grog shops into
> every section of the city, many native American white Protes-
> tants concluded that the ragged edges of the city housed an alien
> and dangerous population composed of chronically idle native
> whites, racially inferior blacks, and unassimilable foreigners—the
> latter, more often than not, attached to the Catholic church.
> What was in fact the most mobile segment of a generally unstable
> urban population now appeared to be permanent, alien, and ubiq-
> uitous. As it encroached on the limited supply of available jobs
> and living space it seemed to threaten the welfare of the entire
> city.[3]

It is important to emphasize the obvious fact that this description of conditions and attitudes in the 1840s and 1850s is strikingly similar to perceptions of urban America in the 1960s, with European immigrants playing the part later filled by black migrants. The comparison is closer yet, for the riots of the 1960s paralleled the disturbances of the 1840s and 1860s, though the earlier uprisings were focused on or initi-ated by Catholics, predominantly Irish, rather than being uprisings against property by Afro-Americans. A common result, too, was the impetus given to the middle class to insulate itself spatially from the problems of urban poverty.

The segregation of cities by class in America has been so pervasive that it has inspired the major school of urban theory stemming from the concentric-zone hypothesis of Ernest W. Burgess.[4] Burgess, and others building on his ideas but finding growth patterns in sectors or multiple nuclei rather than concentric zones, analyzed cities in terms of the spatial separation of economic functions from each other and from residential areas. They divided the residential areas into such catego-ries as "Low-class Residential," "Medium-class Residential," "High-class Residential," "Residential Suburb" and "Commuters' Zone." There is disagreement about the shape those zones take, but not about the basic principle that residential areas are segregated by class. Some have argued that class and ethnic segregation make possible national stability and political cohesion.[5] Others point out that classes are not always segregated in Europe, where traditions of deference and dress define social classes, but that in America residential location is one of the important indicators of class status and thus is guarded jealously.[6] As Amos H. Hawley puts it, "The differentiation of residential areas is to a very large extent a spatial manifestation of social stratification. Social distances tend to be expressed in physical distances."[7] By the eve of World War II the pattern was clear; the turbulence of the nineteenth century had been solved by separation, to the relief of the historian who described the earlier fluidity:

> . . . broad areas on the periphery tended to be made up of people of similar income and class status. . . . On the periphery as in the center, then, metropolitanites of the 1920s and 1930s lived in fairly well-defined neighborhoods among people like themselves. Seldom in their daily activities did they meet strangers who posed a threat to their values, attitudes, or sense of place and community. Thus, the spatial separation of cultural groups and socioeconomic classes limited the opportunities for violent conflict in the modern city.[8]

Following the Second World War, urban housing expanded enormously with the mushrooming of the suburbs. Furthermore, during the 1950s and 1960s, four million black Americans left the farm for the cities and found themselves crowded into ghettoes, excluded from the suburbs. "Between 1950 and 1966, 70 percent of the increase in the nation's white population occurred in suburbs, while 86 percent of the increase in the black population took place in central cities."[9]

The new suburbs clearly maintained and increased the historic separation of classes and races; they also represented a new departure in American urban history because for the first time that separation of classes and races was massively supported by governmment. A variety of devices employed by governments at all levels promoted suburban development and aided the suburbs in excluding the poor and nonwhites. Those devices, supported by a host of private arrangements, were adopted by different governments at different times without apparent consultation or coordination, but their purpose and effects were so uniform that they must be considered as constituting a metropolitan system of protected privilege that excluded lower classes. Zoning, which became popular in the 1920s, grew into an effective weapon for the preservation of class and racial distance. Zoning was justified as a health and safety measure, but criteria presented as protecting health were in fact used to regulate class composition. Minimum lot size, for example, could easily be raised to exclude all but the well-to-do. Anthony Downs notes that, "In Connecticut in 1967, over half of all residentially zoned vacant land in the state was for lots of one-or two-acre minimum size."[10] Zoning laws also insured high-cost dwellings by requiring minimum floor space, minimum room size and minimum set-backs.[11] Multifamily buildings were frequently prohibited, excluding renters who are often disproportionately lower class. Building codes could also be used to add to housing costs and to exclude lower classes.[12]

Zoning has become an object of substantial litigation and criticism in the last decade, but to little avail. A critical awareness, however, has been growing. *Social Action* editorialized, for example, "Zoning has become perhaps the most effective weapon in the defense of this fortress of class homogeneity."[13] Paul Davidoff and Neil Gold, writing in the *Yale Review of Law and Social Action,* sharply condemned the use of zoning for homogeneity: "Exclusionary zoning is largely responsible for the fact that segregation by race and economic class has, over the past few decades, become accepted social policy in large metropolitan areas around the nation. What is special about the use of zoning to this end is that it is accomplished through public law."[14] The impact can be pervasive, as Arthur Lazerow concludes, "Exclusion of low income families from suburbia contributes unmistakably to the racial and economic imbalance in American society. The New York Regional Planning Association, for instance, has estimated that a family with an annual income of less than $15,000 (in 1969 dollars) cannot afford to live in the suburbs of New York City, yet ninety percent of New York City residents are in this economic category."[15]

Government not only uses its power to protect suburbs from lower classes, thus giving them the enormous indirect subsidy of escaping their share of the local tax burden for education and other services which the poor require but cannot fully fund through their taxes, but also gives the suburbs more direct subsidies as well. Federal funding of highways helped make possible the highway system which was essential for the growth of modern suburbs, a multi-billion dollar benefit serving the suburbanites but funded by the nation as a whole. Another enormous subsidy is the tax deduction for mortgage payments. Tax deductions save a family with a median income about twenty cents of every dollar paid on mortgage interest, but a family with a $200,000 income saves seventy cents per dollar.[16] The advantage to the wealthy suburbanite, compared to the middle-income city or suburban home-owner, is obvious. The relative cost to renters, as lower-class families more often are, is greater still since they receive no such subsidy at all. Downs describes the disparity and the total impact of this mortgage interest subsidy:

> The United States Treasury estimates that this subsidy equaled about $5.7 billion in 1971 alone—more than *double* all other housing subsidies combined. In 1966, owner-occupant families with incomes over $100,000 received an average benefit of $1,144 from this subsidy—or 18 times as much as the $64 average benefit received by owner-occupants with median incomes, and 381 times as much as that received by the poorest owner-occupant households. In fact, 69 percent of the total benefit was received by households with incomes of more than $10,000—the upper half of the income distribution.[17]

The notorious Federal Housing Authority tradition of supporting racial and class homogeneity by refusing to insure mortgages in mixed or changing neighborhoods is well-known. J. John Palen notes, "From the 1930s to the present an indirect effect of the FHA program has been to subsidize suburbanization. The suburban tract developments that surround all our larger cities would have been impossible without the federal mortgage insurance programs that, in effect, paid middle-class whites to desert the central cities for newly built government-insured houses with low interest and low down payments in the suburbs."[18] Urban renewal is similarly recognized as a force favoring middle-class interests, often at the expense of the poor, which replaces low cost housing with high cost housing or commercial development.[19]

The total impact of all these private and public policies has been the concentration of the poor, particularly minority poor, in the central cities, in conditions so crowded, with so few job opportunities and so few public resources available, that for them the traditional routes of mobility no longer apply, neither for jobs nor for housing. Meanwhile, the middle and upper classes have been effectively isolated from those problems and, in suburbs, are able to enjoy the economic and cultural advantages of the city without paying their share of the overhead. This metropolitan system itself amounts to the largest subsidy of the well-to-do by the poor. In sum, what has happened in modern America, particularly since World War II, is a formalization of an old tradition of segregation by class. What is different about this new segregation, besides the shift of the areas of low-cost housing from the periphery to the central city, is the massive use of law and public subsidies to maintain the segregation, and the degree to which the migration of less affluent blacks and other minorities adds the factor of race to what had been predominantly a class and ethnic pattern. It is important to remember that segregation by race is more complete, more absolute than was the earlier separation of classes. To ignore this history is to understand the situation today in terms of racial and ethnic conflicts exclusively and to mask the underlying role of class differences.

Today, most white ethnics fall somewhere between the poles of poor inner-city resident and wealthy suburbanite, though they are represented in both groups. Residents of white ethnic neighborhoods may believe they enjoy advantages by excluding the minority poor; in reality, they suffer grievously from a metropolitan system which drains resources from the city to the suburbs—jobs, new housing, and public resources needed for neighborhood preservation. The ethnic neighborhoods face high taxes and the relentless expansion of the ghetto population which, denied opportunities for dispersal which the ethnics themselves have enjoyed, is forced to house its growing population in contiguous white neighborhoods. Though their positions in the system are significantly different, and the white ethnics are relatively advantaged, both blacks and white ethnic groups are victims of the metropolitan system which pits them against one another in bitter but futile and distracting conflict.

If the metropolitan system is this inequitable and this damaging to so many people, one must ask why it has been allowed to develop and to continue in place for so long, and why it has received so much governmental support. One obvious answer is that it persists because it brings enormous advantages to many powerful groups. That may be the key issue, but there are other factors involved as well. The system has seemed to work for many, including the white ethnics who may have become its victims, and it fits well with American traditions of individualism and upward mobility. The basic rationale for the system of class segregation in housing is that classes are not supposed to be permanent. Individuals are expected to move from one segregated section or zone to another until they achieve the American dream of a comfortable suburban home—the reward for hard work and achievement and the symbol of upward mobility. This housing path, a step-by-step succession from slum to suburb, has worked for many white ethnics. Many others, however, are still living in "intermediate" urban neighborhoods, and it is not certain whether they do so by choice or from economic necessity, though some evidence suggests that many do so by deliberate choice.[20] Despite their earlier battles to escape the slums, and the hardships accompanying the changeover of their neighborhoods from white to black, many white ethnics still have benefited from the path of succession and have enjoyed a wide variety of relatively attractive housing choices. Some groups, particularly Jews, have used those opportunities to recreate ethnic communities in the suburbs.[21] For those remaining in the large cities, however, the system now works against them.

If the "trickle-down policy" of homes and neighborhoods has provided some choices and housing for white ethnic groups, how well has it worked for black Americans? The sad answer is that it has hardly worked at all. White ethnics have had some opportunities to find housing in a variety of neighborhoods. One indication of the extent of those opportunities is that seldom has any "ethnic" neighborhood contained over 60 percent residents of any one ethnic group, and today few are even that dense.[22] But as soon as Southern black migrants entered a Northern city in significant numbers, they were confined to neighborhoods that were virtually entirely black. Karl and Alma Taeuber have devised a segregation index, showing the proportion of a population group which would have to move to achieve a random distribution of their housing. They found that for 207 cities in 1960 the segregation index for all regions was 86.2, meaning that 86.2 percent of black households would have had to move in order to achieve the housing distribution expected if race were not a factor. Their study of patterns of segregation from 1940 to 1960 showed almost no change.[23]

Virtually every map of housing in large cities shows the same racial pattern. Black residents are concentrated almost entirely in central cities, in the oldest, most decayed, most crowded housing. Decade by decade the maps show the black areas expanding into contiguous neighborhoods which quickly become entirely black.[24] Instead of passing along the path of succession from the zone of lowest quality housing to the zone of next higher quality housing and, perhaps, eventually to the suburbs, black housing growth simply expands the ghetto, taking over the next "highest" zone of housing entirely and often crowding into the limited supplies of housing available, thereby increasing density and social problems. Therefore, as black housing areas expand, the housing quality does not necessarily improve. White resistance to black entrance into white neighborhoods and a lack of financial resources create a constant shortage of housing for blacks, so that overcrowding and the consequent accelerated decay—aggravated by the fact that blacks usually begin with the oldest and least desirable housing which whites are most willing to surrender—are almost inevitable. The path of succession simply has not worked for black America. Suburbs, except for a few aging areas which have become part of the contiguous ghetto and a few predominantly black suburbs, are almost entirely closed to black residents, even those who have the necessary income.[25]

The result of the subsequent crisis-level shortage of housing for blacks in large, especially Northern, cities has been disastrous for both

black and white neighborhoods. The black population lives, to too
great a degree, in crowded and decaying neighborhoods which engen-
der social conditions that work against the development of effective
neighborhood communities. (Most cities have middle and upper-class
black neighborhoods of excellent quality, but they are far smaller than
needed and are not available to poor or working-class families.) There
is very likely an increased tendency for individuals to try to solve the
problem of poor neighborhoods by moving, and that often means moving into contiguous white areas. These are often the zones of succession
into which working-class white ethnics have moved and where they
have established neighborhoods, yet the effective exclusion of blacks
from other parts of the city and from the suburbs makes these contiguous white ethnic neighborhoods almost the only place the black population can go. Thus the absence of metropolitan-wide housing accessi-
ble to blacks puts destructive pressures on both black and white ethnic
neighborhoods. The housing shortage for blacks tends to pit them and
ethnic groups against one another, as blacks seek the main avenue of
expansion available to them and the white ethnics cry invasion. Neighborhood and school desegregation provide the most graphic examples
of this racial conflict which in the past has included large-scale violence.[26] Two of the least advantaged groups in the population are thus
set against each other in bitter conflict, distracting them from their
common problems of a dearth of economic and housing resources and
indifferent or hostile public policies.

Their most fundamental and common problem with respect to housing is the whole metropolitan system of subsidized, segregated housing
for the middle and upper classes which has limited the housing available to both working-class whites and especially blacks, and at the
same time made those groups pay higher costs for whatever housing
and public services they do receive. White ethnic neighborhoods adjacent to black ghettoes are more easily written off by financial institutions and by the government. Higher city taxes, paying for costs the
suburbs have escaped, drain resources that might be used for neighborhood maintenance. Financial problems make it difficult for cities to
provide adequate services to neighborhoods. Meanwhile, the system of
subsidized housing for the well-to-do gives them not only financial and
housing advantages, but helps them support better schools and maintain easier access to preferred jobs. Class advantages are thus institu-
tionalized by the metropolitan system and the privileges of one generation are handed down to the next, all with the aid of systematic
government support.

The system of class and racial segregation, with upper-income white
housing frequently beyond city borders, helps create ghetto slums and

pits its residents against already weakened white ethnic neighborhoods in competition for housing and scarce governmental resources. The results are disastrous, but the causes are often misperceived. Blacks tend to blame white ethnic racism, a real but not the controlling factor, and the latter tend to blame the former for bringing crime and decay, an exaggerated perception based on some fact since (although new black residents tend to be of the same economic status as previous white residents, and thus not likely to be any more prone to crime than the whites they replace) crime rates do sometimes go up as neighborhoods change.[27] Probably crime increases when the changing neighborhoods are adjacent to large ghettoes, as they usually are, and although the new black residents may not be more crime-prone, their presence may make lower-income black youth more comfortable entering the neighborhoods and engaging in criminal behaviors. Whites seldom stop to consider such possibilities and fear that the entrance of black residents, even in suburbs far from ghettoes, will bring a crime wave.[28] Whites tend to associate crime with race, instead of with class, and oppose the introduction of even middle-class black families.

The causes of street crime are complex, but certainly class is a prominent factor; to associate crime with race rather than with the alienation prompted by persistent poverty is a form of racism, one of the dangerous concomitants of ignoring the class dimensions of what may appear to be racial and ethnic conflict. The idea that crime is a deterrent to neighborhood desegregation simply accentuates the extent to which class factors, rather than race, are central to street crime. It points to the reality that as long as there are sharp differences of class along with massive poverty, neither poor nor working-class areas will be comfortable. Both groups, black and white ethnic, working class and poor, have a common interest in alleviating poverty to protect their neighborhoods.

It seems obvious, though something of a taboo to mention, that as long as there is extreme class differentiation, particularly a massive deprived population living in poverty and near-poverty, neighborhood instability and trauma will persist. The poor and the lower-middle class (most often, in this context, minority and white ethnic groups) will be the front-line sufferers, but the whole middle class will be affected by urban decay, welfare costs, crime, a declining tax base, and a host of other now-familiar problems which are based on the existence of urban poverty. Trying to shape a neighborhood policy in the context of this massive deprivation can only be a matter of searching for ways to contain the poor, or perhaps scatter them in such small concentrations that the historic class and racial objections can be minimized. Neighborhood policy would be, as it actually now is, a matter of protecting the neighborhoods of the non-poor and, in effect, destroying the neighborhoods of the poor either by overwhelming them with density or scattering them so widely as to make significant neighborhood formation impossible.

Neighborhood policy might, by this argument, seem almost irrelevant until the problem of poverty, with the attendant divisive issues of crime and, perhaps, culture, is grappled with effectively. Such may be the case, and it might be best for those concerned with neighborhoods to direct their energies first to lessening class extremes; but it might also be possible for neighborhood policy itself to offer some support for the reduction of the extreme divisions of class. For example, one's neighborhood more and more controls one's access to mobility, through the quality of schools, proximity to jobs (such as are available), and transportation. Central city poor are increasingly locked into the lower classes by poor public education, lack of jobs in the central city, and transportation networks that do not make commuting to jobs elsewhere a practical possibility. Neighborhood planners often seek to improve central city schools and attract jobs, with relatively little success thus far. As has been shown, dispersion of the poor to areas with good schools and more plentiful jobs meets passionate resistance and the decisive power of suburban zoning boards, not to mention bank loan officers or local housing contractors, both of whom usually refuse to provide the resources necessary for the poor to relocate.

Although a satisfactory solution to problems facing neighborhoods requires a greater democratization of resources—so that poverty or near poverty is not an obstacle to neighborhood residents making their own choices about the kind and location of housing they wish, and neighborhoods do not deteriorate because residents cannot afford to maintain their homes—such a solution, tragically, seems to be a long time in the future. Without forgetting that basic goal, we should perhaps work on some more modest, intermediate solutions in the short run. These proposals should be framed so that they are likely to lead to ever greater reforms, not foreclose the probability of further change. A modest beginning might be a dispersed community strategy by which low-rise developments of low-cost housing, large enough to sustain a minimal neighborhood in social and interpersonal terms, could be scattered throughout vacant areas or the unsettled edges of suburbs. These dispersed communities would not be large enough to support their own schools, so students would attend suburban schools, but would have a homogeneous neighborhood as a psychic, cultural support system. The communities should be sited to insure accessibility of jobs. This approach raises serious possible problems such as sanctioning the manufacture of little ghettoes; increasing conflict on the borders and in the schools; stigmatizing the children from the communities; and the possibility that the communities would eventually become a strong force for assimilation and the destruction of their residents' culture. Those difficulties might well prove so serious as to make the strategy unadvisable, but the idea may merit study. In any event, the goal would not be to disperse all blacks into such new neighborhoods. Rather, the new neighborhoods would provide an additional option for black families. Most would likely remain in central city neighborhoods and a few would be dispersed throughout the metropolitan area, though much firmer enforcement of anti-discrimination laws is clearly required in order to provide blacks with something like the variety of housing choices other groups have enjoyed to a greater extent. The new neighborhoods might help reduce crowding in central cities, lower rents by limiting demand, and reduce the pressure on white ethnic neighborhoods by giving blacks another source of housing.

Some of the advantages of such dispersed communities would include access to major resources—jobs, schools and other community services. They would put two groups of people in contact with diversity. Each would be exposed to the other, but would at the same time have the benefit of a "home base" which was relatively homogeneous in terms of each group's traditional associations. The benefits of encounters with diversity, as described by Richard Sennett, Jane Jacobs and Lewis Mumford, would be there to a degree without plunging individuals into completely unfamiliar, possibly alien surroundings.[29] It might happen that each group would begin to adapt some elements of the other's culture, the middle class learning some of the openness and understanding often common among the poor, and the poor picking up some of the middle class's academic values and skills. An exchange of less desirable traits is not likely because community pressures would probably resist them. There is evidence that integrating new communities by class and race increases tolerance and acceptance of such diversity.[30]

The idea of developing dispersed communities for the residents of overcrowded, decaying central city areas is only one possible strategy. Andrew Greeley, for example, suggests a mixture of eight different policies as a way of achieving similar goals, and many of them appear to deserve consideration. They are presented in summary here simply to suggest the range of intermediate policies which could be attempted:

. . . (1) tax credit-subsidized rehabilitation of existing housing stock; (2) metropolitan voluntary housing integration reinforced through the use of a tax deduction mechanism; (3) property value insurance; (4) assistance to local communities in developing self-protection programs; (5) dispersion of public housing and of the

welfare poor until such time as a guaranteed family income can
replace the welfare program; (6) metropolitan voluntary "integration" of schools as a substitute for forced busing confined to
areas within the city limits; (7) effective requirements for mortgage institutions to reinvest in the communities from which they
have drawn their savings deposits; and (8) a coherent development policy for empty land tracts within city limits.[31]

Ironically, despite Greeley's passionate opposition to busing for desegregation and his empty recommendation for voluntary integration
of schools—which obviously has meant historically only continued segregation—metropolitan-wide busing apparently can be an effective
stimulus to housing desegregation. Black parents move nearer their
children's new schools and whites realize there is no place to flee. The
process thus far, however, has been shown to work only in intermedi-
ate-sized cities.[32] Greeley's suggestions seem valuable otherwise, but
they are not likely to be effective unless combined with stronger measures to disperse low-income housing and rebuild central cities with
lower density housing for low-income groups. His stress on voluntarism ignores the importance many attach to the status of an "exclu-
sive" neighborhood devoid of working-class or minority residents.
Anthony Downs has developed a program for dispersing low-income
housing which goes further than Greeley's and relies heavily on increased subsidies for private construction of dispersed low-income
housing and metropolitan-wide policy control, using the power of state
government to overcome local resistance and fragmented
governments.[33]

It is hard to conceive of any program to deal effectively with central
city deterioration and crowding that would not include opening opportunities for low-income housing in other parts of the metropolitan area.
Similarly, it is hard to imagine a way of taking the pressure off white
ethnic neighborhoods without reducing central city crowding and reha-
bilitating central city housing. (The purpose would not be to keep
these neighborhoods all white—they have never been "pure"—but to
end their role as prime targets for black expansion.) Even with those
pressures removed, many white ethnic neighborhoods would need help
to maintain their older housing. In short, any solution to the problems
of urban neighborhoods will require large amounts of money for new
housing and the rehabilitation of existing supplies. The alternatives
are frightening. As Leo F. Schnore writes, "It would seem that, in the
absence of heroic measures, the city will be a conglomerate of poverty-
stricken black cores surrounded by white rings of affluence."[34]

Perhaps the problem of jobs is an even more important one for the
future of neighborhoods. Though jobs have not been the focus here,

they are crucially related, and the history of employment is much like the history of housing with the expectation of upward mobility through a succession of ever better jobs. Indeed, jobs and neighborhood often go together as the better employment opportunities are increasingly found in the suburbs or in central business districts at the end of suburban commuter routes. People excluded from better neighborhoods tend to be excluded from the more desirable jobs, and people excluded from these jobs lack the resources to locate in better neighborhoods. Thus the privileged hierarchy of jobs is linked to the hierarchy of neighborhoods. The low unemployment rate and high quality of work performed by black and white migrants from the South during World War II, as well as a reduced crime rate, show what a striking difference full employment at good wages can make. The "culture of poverty" proved no obstacle to productive work when workers were needed and wages were good. The major cause of poverty is the lack of good jobs, the historic failure of the laissez-faire economic system to provide full employment. The private economy has demonstrated its incapacity to provide full employment again and again. Yet without full employment, the suffering of people and of neighborhoods will continue to be enormous. Here is another area where massive government intervention, perhaps including major restructuring of some sectors of the economy, is needed. In the long run, the basic issues of class, poverty and democracy must be entertained seriously through effective action if stable neighborhoods and a stable society are to persist. Mass poverty in the cities is destructive for the poor, for the white ethnic neighborhoods, for the cities themselves and for the nation as a whole.

It is difficult to find the funds required to solve the interrelated problems of housing and jobs. The current political climate promises reductions, not increases, of federal aid. If the economy were to improve, the job picture and ultimately the housing picture might be helped, but the economic expansion would have to be enormous, on the order of what happens during war, to bring the unemployed and underemployed central city residents into jobs good enough to enable them to compete for good housing. Even then, serious problems of racial resistance would remain. It is very likely that a planned, well-funded government program is the only effective approach possible. It does not seem likely in the current climate, but it should still be advocated. A current campaign might build support and help refine ideas and proposals so that when the political winds do shift, there will be a clear, effective set of proposals with an organized constituency ready for action. That constituency should include all minorities, white ethnic groups, labor, city governments, professional groups and general liberal or reform groups.

I have argued that profit-seeking private actions alone are simply not adequate to the tasks of developing and protecting neighborhoods, providing satisfactory housing, achieving full employment at good wages or achieving a truly democratic control of society. The implication is that the people as a whole, acting through their elected representatives, will have to assume a larger role in managing social policy if those goals are to be achieved. There is another, less satisfactory and narrower, argument for government action to resolve the problems of the class stratification of neighborhoods at the expense of poorer neighborhoods. It is the determinate but widely accepted notion that the government has a special responsibility to solve problems it has created. (The unfortunate distinction between *de facto* and *de jure* school segregation is the most common example, though if segregation damages students it ought to be irrelevant what caused the segregation.) Limiting consideration to such narrow grounds strengthens the case for massive government action to provide equality of housing opportunity because, as I have argued, governments at all levels have been massively and decisively involved in creating the present metropolitan system. Exclusionary zoning, mortgages subsidized through the tax system, federal highway programs to provide transportation to suburbs, discriminatory FHA policies, exploitative urban renewal and their cumulative interaction have produced an inequitable system of housing and neighborhoods through which the government transfers resources from poorer neighborhoods to wealthier ones, and helps upper classes maintain their advantages through favored access to jobs and education as well as to housing. Governmental policy, legislative and administrative, has been essential to the growth and perpetuation of the metropolitan system of housing privilege. On these grounds alone, the government has a legal and moral obligation to do whatever needs to be done to remove the effects of decades of accumulated privilege sponsored by government intervention, and thus to equalize the opportunities for neighborhoods.

Even this narrowly-based call for massive government support for neighborhood revitalization and extensive construction of low-income housing, not to mention the suggestion of major restructuring of the economy to insure full employment, goes far beyond what the current political climate would allow. But the twenties were followed by the thirties; the fifties by the sixties. We can hope the future will bring another shift toward greater governmental intervention on behalf of social justice, and the role of scholars should include hastening that day and preparing better, more fundamental, and more carefully planned programs than were available in the earlier days of reform. Those earlier efforts, important as they were, left major problems unresolved, particularly for the poorest quarter of the population. A better analysis of our needs and possibilities is required so that future reform eras do not have similar failings. A first step is to point to the common interests of racial minorities and white ethnic groups so that they are more likely to unite in support of fundamental change than to quarrel over the division of inadequate resources.

NOTES

[1] Andrew M. Greeley, *Neighborhood* (New York: Seabury Press, 1977), p. 100.

[2] Richard Krickus, *Pursuing the American Dream: White Ethnics and the New Populism* (Bloomington, Ind.: Indiana University Press, 1976), Chapter 7.

[3] Zane L. Miller, *The Urbanization of Modern America* (New York: Harcourt Brace Jovanovich, 1973), p. 47.

[4] For a survey of these theories see J. John Palen, *The Urban World*, 2nd ed., (New York: McGraw-Hill, 1981), pp. 103-123.

[5] Miller, op. cit., p. 154.

[6] Brian J. L. Berry, *The Human Consequences of Urbanization* (New York: St. Martin's Press, 1973), pp. 118-119.

[7] Amos H. Hawley, *Urban Society: An Ecological Approach*, 2nd ed., (New York: John Wiley & Sons, 1981), p. 199.

[8] Miller, op. cit., p. 153.

[9] Howard P. Chudacoff, *The Evolution of American Urban Society* (Englewood Cliffs, N.J.: Prentice-Hall, 1975), p. 247. See also Robert B. Zehms and F. Stuart Chapin, Jr., *Across the City Line: A White Community in Transition* (Lexington, Mass.: D.C. Heath, 1974).

[10] Anthony Downs, *Opening Up the Suburbs: An Urban Strategy for America* (New Haven: Yale University Press, 1973), p. 49.

[11] Downs, ibid., pp. 48-50; Arthur S. Lazerow, "Discriminatory Zoning: Legal Battleground of the Seventies," *American University Law Review*, 21(September 1971): 157-183.

[12] Downs, ibid., p. 50. See also Charles M. Lamb and Mitchell S. Lustig, "The Burger Court, Exclusionary Zoning, and the Activist-Restraint Debate," *University of Pittsburgh Law Review*, 40(Winter 1979): 169-226; Edward P. Welch, "Civil Rights—Public Housing—Tenant Assignment and Site Selection Policies of Municipal Housing Authority Based Upon Racial Criteria Warrant the Imposition of an Interdistrict Remedial Plan," *Villanova Law Review*, 21(December 1975): 115-131; Richard F. Babcock and Fred P. Bosselman, *Exclusionary Zoning: Land Use Regulation and Housing in the 1970s* (New York: Praeger, 1973); Frank A. Aloi, Arthur Abba Goldberg and James M. White, "Racial and Economic Segregation by Zoning: Death Knell for Home Rule?" *Toledo Law Review* I(Winter 1969): 65-108; Lawrence G. Sager, "Questions I Wish I Had Never Asked: The Burger Court in Exclusionary

Zoning," *Southwestern University Law Review*, 11:2(1979): 509-544; but compare Jerome G. Rose, "Myths and Misconceptions of Exclusionary Zoning Litigation," *Real Estate Law Journal*, 8(Fall 1979): 99-124.

[13] Editorial, "Breaking the Noose: Suburban Zoning and the Urban Crisis," *Social Action*, 36(April 1970): 3.

[14] Paul Davidoff and Neil Gold, "Exclusionary Zoning," *Yale Review of Law and Social Action*, I(Spring 1970): 60.

[15] Lazerow, op. cit., p. 161.

[16] Editorial, "Let's Slay Another Sacred Tax Cow," *New York Times* (April 17, 1981), p. 24.

[17] Chudacoff, op. cit., pp. 219, 238-239, 258-259.

[18] Palen, op. cit., p. 272. See also Chudacoff, op. cit., pp. 257-258; Martin Anderson, *The Federal Bulldozer: A Critical Analysis of Urban Renewal, 1949-1962* (Cambridge, Mass.: MIT Press, 1964); Leo F. Schnore, *Class and Race in City and Suburbs* (Chicago: Markham, 1972), pp. 101-102; Robert E. Mitchell and Richard A. Smith, "Race and Housing: A Review and Comments on the Content and Effects of Federal Policy," *The Annals of the American Academy*, 441(January 1979); Hugh O. Nourse and Donald Phares, "The Impact of FHA Insurance Practices on Urban Housing Markets in Transition—The St. Louis Case," *Urban Law Annual*, 9(1975): 111-177.

[19] Greeley, op. cit., passim; Herbert J. Gans, *The Urban Villagers: Group and Class in the Life of Italian Americans* (New York: The Free Press, 1962).

[20] David P. Varady, *Ethnic Minorities in Urban Areas: A Case Study of Racially Changing Communities* (Boston: Martinus Nijoff, 1979), pp. 109-114.

[21] Greeley, op. cit., Chapter 1; Miller, op. cit., p. 46.

[22] Karl E. Taeuber and Alma F. Taeuber, *Negroes in Cities: Residential Segregation and Neighborhood Change* (Chicago: Aldine Publishing, 1965), pp. 28-31, 37-55. See also Stanley Lieberson, *Ethnic Patterns in American Cities* (New York: The Free Press of Glencoe, 1963) throughout for comparison with white ethnic groups and pp. 120-132 on Afro-Americans.

[23] Taeuber and Taeuber, ibid., pp. 256-257; Allan H. Spear, *Black Chicago: The Making of a Negro Ghetto, 1890-1920* (Chicago: University of Chicago Press, 1967), Chapter 1.

[24] Taeuber and Taeuber, ibid., passim.

[25] See Downs, op. cit., Chapters 1 and 2; but compare John Herbers, "Census Finds More Blacks Living in Suburbs of Nation's Largest Cities," *New York Times* (May 31, 1981), pp. 1, 16; and Daphne Spain, John Reid and Larry Long, "Housing Successions Among Blacks and Whites in Cities and Suburbs," Bureau of the Census, *Current Population Reports: Special Studies, Series P-23 No. 101* (Washington, D.C.: 1980). The census study reports that the proportion of blacks in suburbs increased from 4.6 percent in 1970 to 5.6 percent in 1977 (p. 9). Apparently, increasing numbers of middle-class blacks are finding homes in the suburbs, although Palen (op. cit., p. 174) argues that much of the increase is into older suburban areas adjacent to expanding ghettos and does not represent an upgrading of housing. In any case, there is no evidence that suburbs have become an effective alternative to the central city for lower-class blacks.

[26] Among many studies, see particularly the classic commission reports; The Chicago Commission on Race Relations, *The Negro in Chicago: A Study of Race Relations and a Race Riot in 1919* (New York: Arno Press, 1968); and *Report of the National Advisory Commission on Civil Disorders* (New York: Bantam Books, 1968).

[27] Spain, et. al., op. cit., pp. 6-10. Varady, op. cit., pp. 30-31, argues that crime does increase as neighborhoods change from white to black, but that the increase is not a factor in white decisions to move—although he finds studies which show that crime is a factor. Palen, op. cit., p. 113., argues racial change does not bring such deterioration.

[28] Greeley, op. cit., p. 106.

[29] Richard Sennett, *The Uses of Disorder* (New York: Knopf, 1970); Jane Jacobs, *The Life and Death of Great American Cities* (New York: Random House, 1961); Lewis Mumford, *The City in History* (New York: Harcourt, Brace & World, 1961), Chapters 2-5.

[30] Raymond J. Burby III and Shirley F. Weiss, "Public Policy for Suburban Integration...The Case for New Communities," *Urban Law Annual*, II(1976): 101-129; and Helene V. Smookler, *Economic Integration in New Communities* (Cambridge, Mass.: Ballinger, 1976), p. 19 and passim.

[31] Greeley, op. cit., p. 157.

[32] "Wide Busing Programs Are Linked to Increase in Housing Integration," *New York Times* (November 17, 1980), describes a study by Diana Pearce, Director of Research at Catholic University's Center for National Policy Review. The study shows, for example, that Charlotte, North Carolina, is 32.7 percent more integrated now than it was a decade ago when busing began.

[33] Downs, op. cit., Chapter 12.

[34] Schnore, op. cit., p. 1.